About the Author

Sourabh Mukherjee is the author of the true-crime anthology *Death Served Cold* and psychological thriller novels – *The Trail of Blood, The Sinners, In the Shadows of Death* and *The Colours of Passion*, long-listed in WordToScreen, Mumbai International Film Festival, 2018.

India Today has honoured him as one of the "ten celebrated role models of 2022" and Outlook calls him one of the "top ten personalities to look upon if you are looking for an inspiration".

An Electronics and Telecommunications Engineer from Jadavpur University, Kolkata, in his day-job, Sourabh works in a senior leadership role in a global technology firm. He has spoken in global technology summits in London and Las Vegas, as well as at events organized by Bengal Chamber of Commerce and Industry, IIFT, Symbiosis, IIT Guwahati, IIM Lucknow, Kolkata University, among others.

Sourabh has won several literary awards and recognitions, including Golden Pen Award in the Sulekha Monsoon Romance Contest (2014), Juggernaut Selects (2019), Hall of Fame in Literoma International Symposium for Literature and Festival (2020), Speaker in Oxford Bookstores Online Festival (2020). He was awarded the Man of Excellence Award, 2021 by Indian Achievers' Forum for his professional achievements and contributions to nation-building.

: www.sourabhmukherjee.com
: authorsourabhmukherjee
: authorsourabhmukherjee
: sourabhm_ofcl

By the same author

True Crime

Death Served Cold

Thrillers

The Trail of Blood

In the Shadows of Death

The Sinners

Short stories (E-books and Audiobooks)

The Gift

The Cookery Show and a Love Story

A Special Day

Masks

An Autumn Turmoil

The Hunt

The Death Wish

Love Beyond 22 Yards

Crime Beyond 22 Yards

Loves Lost

Appreciation for the author and his works

"Sourabh Mukherjee has emerged as one of the front-runners in Indian crime fiction over the last five years."

- Mid-day

"Mukherjee has left his mark on the genre."

-Deccan Herald

"One of the most popular writers of Indian crime fiction."

- The Asian Age

"Death Served Cold is a compelling read based on true events."

- The Times of India

"In Death Served Cold, the author explores the dark recesses of the female psyche."

- IANS

"Death Served Cold reveals shocking excesses of sadism and aggression rarely associated with women."

- Lokmat Time

"The Sinners is a thrilling work of fiction that weaves together elements of corporate warfare and personal vendetta."

- Yahoo News

"The Sinners is definitely the must-read thriller book of the year."

- The Week

"The Sinners is a gripping and riveting read."

- *Outlook*

"Set in the city of Kolkata, In the Shadows of Death is a fast-paced potboiler which hooks you and keeps you glued to the plot from the very beginning."

- *The Times of India*

"With an almost Freudian understanding of how our childhood experiences influence our adult decisions, Sourabh's novel (In the Shadows of Death) paints a stark picture of urban life in India."

- *The Hindu*

"The theatrical finale comes as much from the extraordinary storytelling as it does from the reveal of the murderer. Mukherjee has the unerring eye of a master craftsman."

- *The Hindu*

"Just when you think you've got it all figured out as per the clues that the killer leaves like crumbs, the author throws you off the path repeatedly with the twists."

-*The News Now*

"A whodunit with several twists, In the Shadows of Death has elements of romance, corporate scandals, and suspense with a strong emotional undercurrent."

- *The New Indian Express*

"A heady concoction of thrill, mystery, psychology and humanity is what makes this book (In the Shadows of Death) such an engrossing fare."

- Punjab Tribune

"In the Shadows of Death is crisp, well-composed and there are no loose ends to irk your mind."

- Yahoo News

"In the Shadows of Death is a page turner till the end with its fluid narrative infused with twists and revelations, which constantly raise your curiosity level."

- Zee News

"A psychological thriller in the true sense of the phrase, In the Shadows of Death delves deep into the psyche of its characters."

- The Free Press Journal

"The character of detective Agni Mitra has been rendered in a very believable and realistic fashion. The author has rummaged into the human psyche and used it as the basis for the detective's theories."

- Tahlka News

"The novel (In the Shadows of Death) explores the city of Kolkata in a way few contemporary novels have attempted. The City of Joy is not just a backdrop but another character in the novel."

- Go-Getter, Go Air in-flight magazine

THE HIGHWAY MURDERS

The True Account of the Killer Who Terrorized the Highways

SOUROBH MUKHERJEE

An imprint of
Srishti Publishers & Distributors

Srishti Publishers & Distributors
A unit of AJR Publishing LLP
212A, Peacock Lane
Shahpur Jat, New Delhi – 110 049
editorial@srishtipublishers.com

First published by
Srishti Publishers & Distributors in 2023

10 9 8 7 6 5 4

This is a fictionalised narrative based on true crimes that happened in India. The real identity of some involved in the cases have been kept under wraps and names of people, places and events have been changed or used fictitiously at some instances.

Printed and bound in India

Dedicated to the sacred memory of
every woman who could never return home.

PART ONE

THE DEVIL STRIKES

Chapter 1

23rd August 2009

Priyamani got off the bus at Adhiyur Road junction. She grimaced as soon as her feet touched the ground. Her feet hurt and there was still a long way to go before she reached home. It was already half past eight in the night.

She had to get on board a bus that went to Erode. However, Erode-bound buses did not stop at the Adhiyur Road junction. She had to find a way of getting to Sengapalli bus stop that was located on the Coimbatore-Erode road. There she would find a bus that would take her home.

As Priyamani waited at the junction for any vehicle that would take her to Sengapalli, the first thought that crossed her mind was that she would finally be able to take her shoes off as soon as she reached home. Next, empty her bladder. A cold shower would be so refreshing. Finally, a hot meal. Priyamani did not remember when she had eaten last. The water bottle she carried in her backpack had been emptied long back. She felt sticky all over in her tight police uniform, thanks to the muggy weather.

It had been a long day, longer than the usual. The Deputy Chief Minister of Tamil Nadu, M.K. Stalin was on a visit to the Tirupur district. Priyamani, who worked in the all-woman police station at Kangeyam in Erode, had been assigned bandobast duty at Valasupalayam Pirivu bus stop on National Highway 47 near the textile industrial city of Perumanallur, as part of the security arrangement for the deputy chief minister.

If there was one thing that Priyamani hated about her job, it was being out on a bandobast duty. It meant having to stand on her feet for long hours without a break. No toilet within miles, no decent food for hours. She usually ended up with an excruciating back ache and sore feet for days. She had flat feet and the kilos she had put on, thanks to erratic work hours and the food from roadside eateries that she had to settle for on most days, did not help either.

Priyamani tried to remember when exactly she had decided to become a policewoman. It must have been in her early teens when she was hooked to those Vijayashanti movies. She had made up her mind early in life that she would grow up to be the nemesis of smugglers, rapists, drug-peddlers, and corrupt politicians who wore garish clothes, sported bushy moustaches and long sideburns, had scars on their faces, their lecherous looks complemented by their devilish laughter. Not everyone in her family had been happy about her decision, but that had not stopped Priyamani from going ahead and fulfilling her dreams. She had always been a strong-willed woman with tremendous faith in her abilities, who believed that one should always listen to one's heart.

Now, at thirty-nine, Priyamani had realised that life on the celluloid was far removed from the reality. In all these years, she had not managed to bust a drug racket, or nab an international smuggler. She had spent most of her life in the force being called in to manage rush-hour traffic on water-logged roads, redirecting traffic during *morcha*s, being on bandobast duty in cricket stadiums or providing security to politicians. That day had been one such.

Priyamani was pulled out of her reverie when she saw a motorcycle approaching the junction. She silently thanked her stars and signalled for a lift. No one would usually refuse a policewoman a lift late in the evening.

When the motorcycle came to a halt a couple of feet away, Priyamani asked the man, "Are you by any chance headed towards Sengapalli?"

The man nodded.

"Can you please drop me at the bus stop?"

The man nodded again and gestured at her to get on the motorcycle. Priyamani said, "Thank you!" and heaved a sigh of relief, as she sat behind him.

The man turned his head and asked gently, "Are you comfortable?"

"Oh yes, I am!" Priyamani could not wait to start.

"That's good," said the man. Then he revved up the motorcycle.

Within seconds, they were speeding down the highway, cutting through the darkness. The wind howling around them, not a word was exchanged between the two strangers.

Chapter 2

"Why did you take this turn?" Priyamani raised her voice above the wind.

The man had turned his motorcycle in the direction of Kalipalayam Road, instead of continuing towards Sengapalli. This part of the road was dark, with most of the streetlights not functioning. It was past 9 p.m. by now. The cold silence of the night was interrupted only by the occasional shrieks of hungry infants inside the few shacks by the road, or the prolonged mournful wails of street dogs. There was not a soul around, as far as Priyamani could see. While the woman inside Priyamani felt nervous, she sought comfort and confidence in the uniform she wore. It was unlikely that anyone would dare to mess with a policewoman.

The man did not bother to respond and continued to speed down the road. By now, the shacks had been left far behind.

Suddenly, the motorcycle stopped.

Priyamani looked around. It looked like a burial ground in the dark. Where had the bastard brought her?

She got off the motorcycle in a flash and weighed her options. She could turn around and take on the man. Or she could run towards the highway. She had a fraction of a second to decide. And she made her decision. That night was not the night to live out her Vijayashanti fantasy. She was too tired and too weak to fight the bully. It made more sense to run. She had to be back on the highway at any cost. The man would not have the gall to chase a policewoman down the highway, for sure.

Priyamani had not run more than a couple of steps when a searing pain shot up from her ankles. She stopped and bent over, barely able to stand on her sore feet now. Her empty stomach churned.

She heard footsteps behind her. As the sound of brisk steps came closer, she could hear the man. He was breathing heavily. Her womanly instincts were on alert immediately. She turned her head slightly and from the edge of her eye, she saw the man behind her, darting at her through the liquid darkness like a raging, salivating bull. She could not see his face in the dark, but she had no doubt now that the man meant harm. Suddenly, she was scared, very scared. The world around her was a haze, and she collapsed on the road.

In no time, there was a strong arm around Priyamani's neck from the back, and the stale breath of the man fanned her face. The bile rose from her empty stomach, and she puked on the man's muscular forearm. Unperturbed, the man began to drag her along the dusty road towards the graveyard. She could barely breathe as the man's arm around her neck cut off the supply of air to her lungs.

Priyamani had not noticed that the man was carrying a machete in his other hand. As they approached the drain near the graveyard, the man struck the first blow on her back with the machete and the blood spurted out. Her neck still in the firm grip of the man, Priyamani let out a muffled cry. The man hit her again, this time on her head. She flailed her arms and legs helplessly, her stifled cries lost in the racket made by a pack of dogs fighting over leftovers in a nearby garbage dump.

Chapter 3

Shankar saw the woman when he was riding past the Adhiyur Road junction on the motorcycle he had stolen from Annadurai the other day. In the faint streetlight, his eyes were drawn to her full body under her tight uniform. He stripped her in his mind, almost as an instinctive reflex. Immediately, he had a throbbing hard-on. As luck would have it, the woman was gesturing at him for a lift!

All through the ride, the warmth of her body brushed against his back, and her womanly smell fanned the fire raging through his veins.

As he now looked at the woman sprawled on the ground, her head and back bleeding profusely, he could not help laughing. So much for the power of the uniform! The bitch had tried to kick at his crotch a few times, but a punch in the gut had tamed her. She had doubled up in pain and urinated in her pants.

Shankar yanked off her pants and her undergarments, soggy from the urine. His fingers now firmly around her neck, he entered her with such force that she closed her eyes tight and let out a guttural cry, tears and blood streaming down her face.

Shankar came inside her after a few thrusts, but the fire inside him showed no sign of dying down. He kept slapping Priyamani till her lips split open and bled. He tightened his grip around her neck and watched her. Her hair dishevelled, eyes engorged, the tongue sticking out, the drool past her lips, her desperate struggle for just one breath – one of the several thousands, which we do not bother to count every day. In no time, he was hard again. He entered her and moved in and out at a frenzied pace, choking her with one hand and fondling her body with the other. He was so enjoying this! There was no bigger pleasure than fucking the law – quite literally.

By the time Shankar had pulled out of her, Priyamani had passed out.

Shankar stood up and lowered his *veshti*. He walked gingerly to where he had dropped his machete a couple of feet away.

He returned to Priyamani's senseless body and made a deep cut across her chest. Then, a couple of cuts along her abdomen. The thighs next. As the blood sprayed him red, Shankar went about his job like a man possessed. When he was finally content, he dropped the machete and allowed himself a few seconds to take in the spectacle before his eyes.

Sitting on his haunches near the dead woman, he pulled off her gold ear studs. The *mangalsutra* with its gold *thali* went next. Finally, he reached into her trouser pockets and pulled out her Nokia phone. A cheap model, but he did not complain.

Shankar stood up and walked a few feet to the motorcycle. He picked up his bag and put the machete back inside. The breeze caressed his face as he looked around. Beyond the far end of the graveyard, there were a few huts, surrounded by trees that looked like patches of ink on the blue-black night sky. But no one would be up for the next several hours. There could not be a better place than the drain to dump the dead cop.

As he looked again at Priyamani's lifeless body, drenched in blood and almost torn into slices, Shankar felt the familiar stirrings in his loin and raised his veshti almost instinctively. He sat down on his knees and parted her legs one last time.

Chapter 4

19th September 2009

A few days back, the inhabitants of the village had started cleaning up the graveyard and the adjacent fields, as the area had become a refuge for hooligans. They gathered behind the dense bushes to drink, gamble and tease the girls who happened to pass by the graveyard on their way to and from the village. The local police acted on complaints filed by the villagers, conducted surprise raids, and made a few arrests now and then. But the miscreants would be back in a few days. The villagers, therefore, had resolved to take matters into their own hands. They decided to clean up the area, remove the bushes, and take turns in patrolling the area all through the day and the night.

Selva had been busy since morning, working at the far end of the graveyard next to the highway. The undergrowth there was dense, and no one usually ventured into that part of the graveyard. Not even the ruffians. Selva, however, was not taking chances. One of the boys had accosted his daughter the other day when she was returning home from school and tried to act smart. He would leave no place for the bastards to hide.

He wiped the sweat from his brow. It was past ten in the morning, and the air was getting warmer. Putting down his spade, he lighted a *beedi* and sat down under a tree. He had taken only a couple of puffs when he noticed the smell. It was a nauseating stench, coming from the direction of the highway.

Selva stood up and walked towards the highway. As he went closer, the stench grew stronger. It must be a dead dog, Selva thought. They always got run over by the trucks speeding down the highway. He could now hear the buzz of flies. Whatever they were after was in the drain that ran along the edge of the graveyard, parallel to the highway.

As Selva peeped into the drain, a shriek escaped his gaping mouth. It was the body of a woman lying inside the drain. Her face was turned to a side. The lower half of her body was naked. She wore a police shirt. Blood had congealed into black patches all over her body. The dogs had eaten away parts of her limbs and her face. It was not difficult to figure out that the body had been there for a long time as it looked heavily decomposed.

Selva stepped back a few inches and supported himself by holding on to the trunk of a tree. He felt giddy and retched a few times. He then turned around, picked up his spade and started running towards the village.

He had to call the police station.

Chapter 5

The call from the village was received at around eleven in the morning. The villagers had found the decomposed body of a woman in a drain near the graveyard. There was a police shirt on the dead woman's body.

In August, Priyamani had not shown up when all the other constables had reported at the police station after their bandobast duty at Perumanallur. Her husband, Manian, had officially reported her missing. Finally, a case had been registered on 30th August and an investigation had been kicked off. Inspector S. Swaminathan had been put in charge. The police had made inquiries, but had failed to gather any useful information regarding her whereabouts. For weeks, Swaminathan had not been able to make any headway. That morning, as soon as the call was received, Swaminathan lost no time and rushed to the spot with his team. His gut told him that this could be the policewoman who had gone missing almost a month back. And his gut was usually never wrong!

When he reached the spot, Swaminathan was surprised to find that the gruesome sight and the unbearable stench had not been able to deter the villagers from gathering around the drain. Even women and children were not ready to miss the ghastly spectacle. Such was the lure of gore!

Covering his nose and mouth with a handkerchief, Swaminathan bent over and looked inside the drain. It was the body of a woman alright, as he had been informed over the phone. There was no doubt that the shirt she had on was part of a uniform. She had bled profusely from her chest and her stomach, as the shirt had dark patches of congealed blood. She was completely naked underneath, suggesting that she might have been sexually violated.

The forensics team got into action and recovered the body. No luck with any telling evidence anywhere in the vicinity. The body had been left in the open for far too long. Animals, birds, insects and field rats had shared the spoils for weeks. There had also been spells of shower over the last several days. Swaminathan asked around in the village, but no one had seen the body before Selva.

The body was sent for an autopsy. Preliminary investigations confirmed Swaminathan's guess.

The woman, indeed, was constable Priyamani.

Chapter 6

Swaminathan was in his office, reading the autopsy report, sipping piping hot masala chai.

The report reaffirmed the fact that Priyamani's body was heavily decomposed. It was estimated that it had been lying in the drain near the graveyard for anything between three and four weeks. Swaminathan made calculations in his mind. The timing did coincide with that of Priyamani's disappearance. The woman had died from multiple fatal wounds on her back, head, chest, stomach, thighs and arms. The wounds appeared to have been inflicted by a sharp weapon. She had been raped multiple times – ante-mortem and post-mortem. The vaginal swabs, however, had not yielded sufficient traces of DNA that could be used for finding a potential match from the police records.

Swaminathan threw the report on the table, and rubbed his face, letting out a deep sigh. He stood up and walked to the window that overlooked the narrow lane next to the police station. There were dark clouds in the horizon, and the air was thick with moisture. It was late in the afternoon, and boisterous girls in uniforms with their plaits neatly tied with coloured ribbons and satchels slung over their backs, ran homewards in small groups from the school across the road. Swaminathan could hear their giggles from his office. He kept looking at the girls, and a chill ran down his spine when he remembered the horrific sight of the woman lying dead in the drain by the highway. The safety of these girls and thousands of others like them was the reason why he got paid every month.

He had failed Priyamani. The entire force had. She had been one of their own.

Swaminathan was proud of his job. Yes, there were a few bad apples. He knew cops who abused the power that the system had bestowed upon them. They took bribes, or worked in collusion with gangsters, unscrupulous businessmen and corrupt politicians. But with few exceptions, the force had men and women who were determined to protect the innocent and uphold the dignity of law. That was what Swaminathan reminded himself every day when he woke up and put on his uniform.

The barbaric rape and murder of Priyamani was not just a crime against a woman, alone and helpless on that night, but Swaminathan saw it as an affront against the police. He was not going to take it lying down.

"I will find the bastard and bring him to task," he whispered to himself. He was simmering with rage.

In the next two hours, Swaminathan assembled a team and had an action plan ready.

Chapter 7

Three days later, Swaminathan was in a meeting with senior officials.

"We have found out from police stations in the vicinity of the highway between Tamil Nadu and Karnataka that there are *at least a dozen unsolved cases of rape and murder*, which were reported over the last twelve months. We have collected the autopsy and forensic reports pertaining to all these cases and have studied them at length. Most of the victims were prostitutes, but we also have women who were not," Swaminathan paused briefly.

Swaminathan had spoken to many of the prostitutes from the areas where there had been murders. There was something about these women and their fates, the circumstances that had made them who they were, which Swaminathan thought he recognised and understood. However, what he could not understand was where their irrepressible optimism came from. They had experienced first-hand the darkest perversions of the human soul, yet they never seemed to lose hope. So, when one of their sisters went missing, they came forward in troops, hopeful that justice would be done. Swaminathan heard them crying and cursing. Some of them cried for those who had been raped and murdered, some considered themselves lucky that they had not met with the same fate, and some had cursed the monster who had raped and killed some of their own. As he spoke, the faces flashed before Swaminathan's eyes.

He said, "The killings are not random. No doubt, there is a pattern. All the bodies were found in drains, graveyards, and empty fields along the highway. In every instance, the woman was brutally raped multiple times, before and often after death. The bodies revealed signs of grievous torture. Split lips, damaged eardrums, signs of strangling, bite marks in private parts. The bodies appeared to have been cut in a frenzy, as if by someone possessed. In one case, the stomach wound was so deep that the woman's intestines had spilled out. I am afraid, there is a serial killer roaming our highways!"

"That makes it easier for us, doesn't it?" quipped Ramaswamy, one of the new recruits.

Swaminathan turned towards him and asked, "What makes you say that?"

"Isn't it easier to find one man who's responsible for a dozen incidents than having to find a dozen different men?" Ramaswamy asked.

Swaminathan smiled and replied, "Let me explain to you why it *isn't* more convenient. When someone commits a premeditated murder, he can create a strong alibi for himself, remove all evidence from the crime scene, dispose of the weapon and so on. We often end up having nothing in our hands that can lead us to a clever murderer. What then comes to our rescue is the *motive*. We examine the likely motive of everyone from a bunch of suspects, and zero in on the perpetrator. In the case of serial killings, while there is a pattern and a similar modus operandi that point to the fact that there is one individual responsible for multiple murders, the murders themselves are random. The lack of a logical motive is the biggest handicap that you run into. Consider this case as an example. While there are a dozen reported cases of rape and murder on the highways which follow a distinct pattern, suggesting that there is a depraved psychopath behind all of those cases, there is no motive behind his actions. Which means, it could be anyone from among the thousands who are travelling up and down these roads every day!

"Also, when we investigate a murder, we usually assume that the victim was known to the murderer. We look at the victim's network – family, friends, colleagues, social acquaintances – to find someone who has a reason to kill. This is not the case in an investigation to find a serial killer."

"Good work, Swami!" exclaimed P. Venkataraman, the Superintendent of Police, Tirupur. He then looked around the room and said, "However, a word of caution. While we all agree with this line of thinking, let us not go to the media with the hypothesis of a serial killer prowling on the highways, unless we are absolutely sure, and are close to getting our hands on him. Otherwise, we will end up creating panic, which we must avoid at all costs. So, do we have a profile of the killer?" he asked, turning again towards Swaminathan.

Swaminathan nodded and said, "We do, sir. As you know, there are usually three kinds of serial killers. The first kind are those whom we call *stationary killers*. They usually lure their victims to one place. It could be a house or a hotel. The second are the *territorial killers*. They usually kill in the same territory. For example, Jack the Ripper committed his murders in red-light areas. The territory for a killer can also be an entire town. In that case, the killer may be active anywhere within that town, making it difficult to trace him. The third kind is the *nomadic killer*, whose victims are spread across cities and states. These are the ones who are most difficult to track down.

"I firmly believe that the perpetrator we are looking for belongs to the third category. He is someone who travels regularly up and down the highway between Tamil Nadu and Karnataka, and possibly to other neighbouring states, targeting vulnerable women along the highway. Some of the women he has raped and killed are sex workers you would usually find near fuel stations and roadside dhabas. He can easily dispose of the bodies. In every case, the body of the victim was found several miles away from where she lived. This means, he probably has his own means of transportation."

"So, what are you planning to do next?" asked the SP. "I am sure you are aware that the media is after us. The more time we take to solve the mystery around Priyamani's murder, the more creative the crime editors in the newspapers will get. There are ridiculous conspiracy theories being published by certain sections of the media already." He looked around the room and added, "There is also political pressure. Do not forget that Priyamani was on bandobast duty on that day for the protection of Mr Stalin. He has been speaking about the safety of women in the state, and then we end up with this shocking incident of rape and murder of one of our own. In fact, in a report published by a leading newspaper, the victim has been referred to as *'Stalin guard'*! We are certainly not looking good."

"Sir, I have alerted the police in all the southern states, as well as in Goa and Maharashtra. Search groups have been assembled, and we have launched a massive manhunt across the western and southern states. We are conducting inquiries in roadside dhabas, oil pumps, toll stations, truck and bus terminals and police *chowkis* for any clue that can lead us to the killer. We have put up barricades and have started checking vehicles on the highways, especially during the night. Our teams are patrolling the villages along the highways. The police from three states are working together.

"I know this is not going to be easy. Police officials from four states are involved in the manhunt. It is possible that not everyone agrees with our theory. The police from other states may have different priorities. There is no standard way of working. There will be communication gaps. There will also be issues with coordination. It is likely that not everyone in the task force will be completely aligned on the developments in the investigation at any given point in time.

"But, sir, we will have to overcome these hurdles. This is, beyond any reasonable doubt, the work of a deranged monster. And I am determined to end the reign of terror on the highways," Swaminathan clenched his fists as he spoke.

PART TWO

THE REIGN OF TERROR

Chapter 8

Maari Muthu was driving his truck down the highway to Karnataka when his son Jaishankar was born in 1977 at Kanniyampatty in the district of Salem in Tamil Nadu.

As a child, Shankar got to see very little of his father, who was out most of the time, driving along the highways across the states of Tamil Nadu, Karnataka, Andhra Pradesh and Kerala. Shankar had often been told that he looked like his father. Everyone called his father Muthu, and so did he. "You don't call your father by his name," his mother Gayathri would tell him, "Call him *appa*."

He remembered his father as the man with a moustache and hair growing past his shoulders, who would spend occasional evenings at home. Sitting by the window, drinking from a bottle, he would tell him stories about his adventures on the dark roads, while his mother would sit in a corner of the small room, cooking rice, *paruppu, sambhar* and *poriyal* for dinner. Shankar would fall asleep listening to the stories, resting his head on Muthu's lap.

Those were the happy memories, and unfortunately, there were not too many of them.

Muthu usually came home in a foul mood, drunk and showering abuses on the world. Shankar could never figure out what made his father angry, and he dared not ask him. For that matter, he did not ask his mother, or his elder brother or his elder sister. He just knew that it was best to stay away from Muthu when he was mad. Muthu would be fishing for a reason to beat him up, however trivial that reason might be. The same fate awaited his mother and his elder siblings on most occasions. Shankar hated seeing his mother being beaten up. She would often end up with a black eye or with scars on her face and body that took weeks to vanish, only to be replaced by fresh ones.

Sometimes, Muthu returned home late in the night, drunk, and locked himself up in the small room by the farm with a woman. Those were women whom Shankar had never seen in the neighbourhood. He stared wide-eyed at their loud make-up and garish clothes of the kind he never saw his mother wear. When he asked Gayathri, he was told that they were Muthu's friends, just as Shankar had friends in school with whom he shared his tiffin and played in the fields. Gayathri served food in the room when Muthu ordered, wiping her tears silently.

Sometimes, Shankar tip-toed to the room and stood outside the closed door, curious about what was going on inside. What games were they playing and why could he not join them? He could even call his mother and his siblings if Muthu allowed him to, and they could form a team! He put his ear on the door, listening to the strange noises that came from the room. He heard sounds of slapping and screaming. Sometimes, they seemed to be crying and moaning, like you did when you were in pain. But weren't they supposed to be playing a game? Why would you cry when you were having fun? Shankar ran to Gayathri, shooting a volley of questions, but Gayathri did not have an answer for any of those questions. She would ask him to sleep and dream of fairies. Shankar obeyed his mother and went to bed, curling up beside her.

But sleep eluded him. He kept thinking about the games Muthu was playing in the room by the farm. His mother lay next to him, hugging him tight, his face hidden in her bosom. Shankar felt the tremors there, as his mother cried all night for reasons he was not allowed to know. All he could do was run his fingers through his mother's hair with the hope that she would stop crying and fall asleep, which she never did. When Shankar finally fell asleep, he dreamt not of fairies, but of the women Muthu played with in the room by the farm, with their crimson red lips and kohl-rimmed eyes.

Muthu's stories had already fired Shankar's fascination about life on the roads. He spent hours watching the highway glide lazily by his house, twisting and turning like a snake up to the horizon. Every time he heard a truck or a bus pass by their house, he used to run out and gape in awe. Gayathri had a tough time keeping an eye on him, and every time he was too close to the road, she would have to leave her work to drag him back into the safe confines of the house.

"Stay away from the roads, Shankar. There is a demon there that will cast a spell on you!" Gayathri warned her son. The little boy meant the world to her, and she did not want to lose him to the highways.

Shankar started working as a farmer, and Gayathri got him married to a fifteen-year-old girl, Rajeshwari, when he was twenty-three. She hoped that matrimony and subsequent fatherhood would keep Shankar away from the roads. She did not want her son to live the nomadic life of a trucker like his father did – keeping bad company and indulging in wine and women. She had failed to keep her elder son away from the roads, but she was determined not to let Shankar follow their footsteps.

Life, however, holds our hand and puts us on the path we are destined to be on. Shankar could not stay away from the roads for long. One fine morning, he ran away from home, leaving behind his wife and his three daughters.

Chapter 9

It was only after Shankar had left his home that he realised how stifled his life had been in that pigeon-hole. All his life, he felt chained and throttled as the empty roads and open skies kept calling him. He had finally managed to break free. He was finally living out the dreams that had been sown in his infant mind by the stories he had heard from Muthu.

No more hiding outside the room by the farm and hearing Muthu fuck the whores he picked up on the highways. No more wiping the tears of his mother through never-ending nights of pain. No more toiling in the farms only to sell his blood and sweat for a pittance. No more putting up with the bickering of his wife in exchange for fifteen minutes of boring sex. No more worrying about the future of his three daughters. He was a free man with the world at his feet! He now had the wind in his hair, and the damp fragrance of the woods lining the roads excited him. He celebrated his nomadic life. It did not bother him that he no longer had a home to return to. He made the world his home. He got drunk like there was no tomorrow and slept in his truck. Sometimes in a farm by the road. Sometimes curling up on a pavement with a stray dog for company.

Before long, the demon of the highways did cast its spell on Shankar.

***

Shankar had not seen the situation as a problem that he should be worried about. It first manifested itself as a heightened interest in sex. Most of the time, after work, Shankar found himself getting drunk and ending up in cheap video parlours or dingy cinema halls that exhibited pornographic films. It was for some time simply a sign of enhanced sexual interest, fuelled perhaps by his new-found freedom and the relaxed frame of mind, away from worldly woes, that came with that freedom. But, over time, that interest began to shift towards matters of a sexual nature that involved violence. For instance, Shankar began to enjoy a violent rape scene on the screen more than watching the heroine dancing in the rain in a clingy wet white saree.

The change was not immediate, but it came about gradually, almost stealthily. At times, he wondered why. Did he have any inherent hatred for women? Did this malice come from watching his father slip into that room by the farm with the women he picked up, leaving his mother to shed tears through the night? He did not know. What he knew for sure was the fact that he was gradually falling prey to a kind of weakness that gave rise to his interest in violent sexual activities, which began to completely absorb his fantasies! Slowly, but surely.

Initially, Shankar did not see *himself* as the one inflicting pain on a woman. He fantasised about those situations. He found gratification from seeing or imagining *others* engaging in such acts of sexual violence. But that changed very soon!

Chapter 10

One night, Shankar stepped out of a watering hole, drunk, barely able to walk. He was headed to a farm where he would put up for the night. As he walked down the narrow dusty road, with houses breathing on each other and inhabited mostly by prostitutes, his eyes went to an open window, and he stopped in his tracks.

There was a woman with her back to the window, undressing.

Shankar stood rooted to the spot with his eyes fixed on the bare back of the woman. It was as if a titillating scene from one of the movies had come to life in front of his eyes. He was turned on instantly, the animal inside him threatening to break free. When the woman was done undressing and then putting on her nightwear, she turned the light off and Shankar walked away. But he could not ward off the lurid images in his mind all through the next day and was back again in front of the same window the next night. He told himself that he meant no harm. He just wanted to *see*. Nothing more.

Before long, it became a habit. He began, with increasing regularity, to get drunk and scan the houses in the neighbourhood all through the night like a ghost, looking for open windows to peep in, to watch a woman undress or take a shower or a couple make love, or whatever else presented itself before his hungry eyes. He gained a tremendous amount of gratification from his voyeuristic behaviour, and with time, became increasingly adept at it – just as anyone becomes adept at something that is done over and over again. He became obsessed with his adventures, and soon he started repeating his search during the early morning hours as well. He was not getting enough sleep. He was continually exhausted, and his tired mind started playing games with him.

As the obsession developed, Shankar could sense a growing conflict between his normal personality, and the monster inside him that demanded more and more attention and craved for the satisfaction of its needs.

Very soon, the tension threatening to tear him apart would reach a point of no return.

***

One evening, as Shankar stepped out of the bar, heavily drunk, he saw a woman passing by. He could tell from her make-up and clothes that she had been waiting for business outside the bar. Since it was late and the bar was about to pull down shutters, she had, in all probability, also decided to wind up for the night. She was alone, and she stepped into a poorly illuminated side street that went to the neighbourhood which Shankar was very familiar with, thanks to his late-night and early-morning escapades. He followed the woman.

In the faint streetlight, his eyes hovered on the woman's sweaty back, bare over her blouse, and the alluring sway of her bottom under her saree. He found himself in the grip of uncontrollable lust, which seemed to completely overwhelm his senses. An urge to *attack* the woman overpowered him, in a way he had never felt in the past! He started looking around for something to attack the woman with.

He picked up a bamboo stick he managed to find by the road. He kept following the woman along the dusty road, having lost control over the salivating monster that was breathing fire, gnawing away at his innards. He was now ready to strike a blow!

Shankar had increased his pace and had started closing the gap between the woman and himself, when the woman suddenly turned to her right, opened the wooden gate of a house and walked inside. Shankar stopped in his tracks, gasping for breath with his mouth open, the sweat streaming down his face. He dropped the stick and stood in front of the house, scared to follow her inside. There were lights in the windows, and he could hear voices inside. He knew that his prey had escaped.

But something had definitely snapped inside him that fateful night. All these days, he had sought gratification in his fantasies of sexual violence, but had never reached the point where he *himself* was so close to harming another human being to satiate his carnal desire.

That night, the monster had won.

Chapter 11

With the revelation from that experience and the recollection of the frenzied desire that had seized Shankar that night, the beast inside him that was obsessed with women and sex and violence finally came out of the darkness where it had been lurking all these days. In the months and years preceding that night, Shankar had passed women in alleys and dark roads, women who were alone and attractive, especially the ones he had seen in various stages of undress on several occasions while making his rounds peeping into windows, but it had never occurred to him that *he* could inflict pain on the woman and have sex forcibly. But that night, a switch had flipped. He had finally succumbed to the tension that had been brewing inside him. A hole had been made in the dam. It had not burst yet, but the cracks were prominent.

Over the next few evenings, Shankar began to hunt the same neighbourhood for other women, constantly playing in his mind the images from the night when the monster had made a breakthrough and he had followed a lonely woman down that street with a stick in his hand.

On one such evening, Shankar saw a prostitute, waiting for business under a flickering streetlight, close to the bar. She wore heavy make-up, her full body barely restrained by her skimpy clothes. Images began to flash in Shankar's mind. He saw his father coming home after days, drunk, his arm around the same woman, tottering to the room by the farm, sounds of laughter from inside, his mother carrying food for them to the shack, his father shouting at her, sounds of laughter again, followed by animal cries of pleasure as the bodies of his father and the whore congealed into a heaving, throbbing mass of sweaty flesh.

Shankar could feel his throbbing hardness. His throat was dry, his lips parched. He walked up behind the prostitute and hit her with the bamboo stick he had been carrying. The woman fell down and started screaming. Shankar panicked as he saw the blood trickling down from the side of her head where he had struck her, down her cheek, by her thick lips painted a shocking red, past her throat, into the deep sweaty cleavage. He looked around, scared, as the woman kept screaming. And then, he started running.

What he had done suddenly terrified him. He did not know where he was headed, but he ran and ran. He was full of remorse. He remonstrated himself as he ran from his unseen adversary. He was horrified by the realization that he *could* attack a woman brutally with intentions of having sex with her. He was afraid of being found out. He was afraid that he would be caught and thrown into a jail where he would rot for the rest of his life.

After its initial victory a few nights back, the monster had lost that night and retreated into its cave. But, for how long would it sleep?

Chapter 12

The sobering effect of Shankar's experience was that the cracks in the dam were mended for some time. He swore to himself that he would not do something like that again. In fact, he would stay away from any activity that might lead him to a similar situation. He did everything that he could to tame the demon inside. He began to drink himself senseless during the nights, so that he could not peep into windows. When he was out drinking, he stayed with friends, and left the bar with them. For weeks, the atrocity of what he had done, and its possible consequences that he had averted that night by a stroke of luck, stuck with him, and he watched his behaviour.

However, this state of sobriety did not last long.

Within a couple of months, the experience had lost its impact, and Shankar was back peeping into windows, slowly slipping back into his old routine. As his fear receded and his desires overpowered him, Shankar had to feed his hunger at any cost. He attempted a logical analysis of the situation and realised that he would just have to be more careful. The last time, his action had been fraught with incredible danger, badly thought out. Instead of allowing himself to fall into a spontaneous, unplanned act of violence like he had done the last time, he would have to think of alternate means of devouring his prey. There had to be a few ground rules.

A few nights later, he saw a prostitute walking home. He followed her, keeping safe distance, controlling his desire to pounce on her on the road. Once she had reached home, he watched her through an open window in her room as she removed her makeup, undressed, took a shower, and went to bed. He walked along the perimeter of the house, looking for a way to get in. At the back of the house, there was a door that opened to the yard. A gentle push on the door and the rickety old catch inside gave away.

Shankar stepped into the silent house.

The woman was asleep in the bedroom. Shankar stood by her bed for a few seconds, watching her full bosom rise and fall in rhythm with her breathing. Then he hit her on the head with a bamboo stick. When he was sure that the woman had fainted, he picked her up. He ran to the highway where he had parked his truck. He tied up her hands and feet and gagged her mouth. He threw her into the back of the truck and covered her up with tarpaulin. He jumped into the driver's seat and started driving.

It was the first time that Shankar had abducted a woman. He was nervous deep down and drove frantically. After a few miles, he stopped. When he looked around, all he could see were empty fields on both sides of the road. Not a soul around. He turned the engine off and leapt out of his truck. Then he dragged the woman out.

The woman had, by then, come to her senses, and cried for help through her gag. Shankar wrapped his fingers around her neck, so that her screams were soon reduced to weak, intermittent muffled noises. He tore off her clothes, untied her feet, and spread her legs apart.

As he moved in and out of the woman in a frenzy, Shankar laughed at the irony of the situation. The woman writhing in pain on the dust by the side of the highway, naked and being brutally violated, was an anonymous, unknown, living, breathing human being. For Shankar, however, she was nothing more than a symbol. A symbol of eroticism, a lurid image, an object of pleasure, something that he had been craving for all these days.

Once Shankar had relieved himself inside the woman, she ceased to be an object of pleasure, and was now a *problem* that he had to deal with. The woman, crying and begging to be let off, was suddenly a threat. Shankar's intoxication had worn off, and his rational self was beginning to surface. It recognised the state of affairs and had to find a way of concealing the act. Shankar convinced himself that the woman had to be killed, and that was not only justifiable, but also necessary for his survival. He could not allow the crime to be detected. He could not allow himself to be captured by the police.

He picked up the bamboo stick and struck a blow on the woman's head with all the force he could muster. He did not miss the crunch of her skull cracking. He kept showering blows on her head. In no time, her face was a bloody muddle of broken bones and squashed flesh.

Chapter 13

As he drove away from where he had left the lifeless body of the woman, Shankar was scared, and wanted to go as far away as he could before the day dawned. The sky was clearing up, and it seemed to Shankar that he had miles to go before he could consider himself safe.

For days and weeks after killing his first victim, Shankar was restless and anxious. He kept wondering if the disappearance of the prostitute had been noticed, if anyone had seen him in the vicinity of her house that night, if the police had been informed, and if the police had managed to find any evidence. The mutilated body must have been found by now and reported to the police. Had anyone identified the body? Had the police been able to establish a link with the disappearance of the prostitute from a town several miles away? He came across as distracted, his mind being preoccupied with his worries. He checked in newspapers, and also watched out for hints in his conversations with truckers from the area.

There had been nothing to worry about, so far.

***

During those moments of anxiety and uncertainty about a possible police investigation into the mysterious disappearance of the woman and the discovery of the battered body of a rape victim on the highway, guilt and remorse did try to raise their ugly heads, but as the monster reasserted its force, such feelings were quashed for good.

Before long, Shankar stopped dwelling on the past, and began to look forward to his next adventure.

And the next. And then, the next.

He cherished each one of the prostitutes he had picked up and assaulted, gagged and tied, raped and killed – the same pattern repeated almost every time. He remembered one or the other every time he closed his eyes and ran his fingers along the sharp edge of the machete, which he always carried in a black bag. He remembered her inviting eyes when he had approached her. He remembered the naughty smiles and raunchy words, with which she had been enticing prospective customers. He remembered how she had resisted being fucked, gagged and tied, when she was, in reality, in the business of getting fucked in whichever manner her client pleased, in exchange for money. He remembered the smells of betel leaves, sweat and cheap perfume that had filled his nostrils as he had mounted her. He remembered every fruitless attempt she had made to hold on to life as his fingers around her neck had sunk in deeper, the look of unbelieving horror frozen in those eyes for an eternity. He remembered how her face had changed colours – from a warm red one moment to a cold deathly white the next. Her skin had felt warm and smooth when he had played with her body, and cold and rubbery after she had died. He remembered how she had been his object of pleasure one moment, and in the next, a corpse ready to be kicked into a ditch to be devoured by dogs and rats.

Experience kept teaching Shankar. Over a period of time, there was less panic, less confusion, and even lesser fear and apprehension about being caught. Shankar figured out that public hysteria and consequent police activity would be triggered by only one thing – the discovery of the body. Without a body, police investigations did not progress, publicity died a natural death, and suspicion was averted. Therefore, the women would be removed from wherever they stayed or hung out, and dumped somewhere far away with their faces and bodies mutilated beyond recognition, and he himself would disappear from the scene of crime in a very short time.

More and more disfigured bodies of women began to be discovered in open fields, graveyards, and farms along the 'highway of terror'.

Chapter 14

It was late in the afternoon and the heat was sweltering. When you looked at the road ahead, the hot air on the asphalt made everything look like it was floating. Shankar had been driving since the morning. He was hungry and his mouth was parched. He had run out of his supply of water long back.

When he saw the dhaba by the road, he parked his truck by the edge of the road and turned off the engine. As he leapt out of the truck and wiped the sweat off his face, his eyes went to one of the benches in front of the dhaba. There was a woman sitting there by herself, eating absent-mindedly.

Shankar ordered a thali and a glass of butter-milk, and took a seat close by. His eyes were on the woman. He wanted to check if she was going to be joined by anyone else. After a while, he was certain that the woman was alone. And probably, depressed for some reason. When the kid brought his order, he asked him to put the food on the table next to the woman's.

As he ate, Shankar started talking to the woman, first about the torturous summer that year, then about the lack of safety on the highways, slowly moving on to more personal topics such as the pains of a trucker's life, the difficulties of having to stay away from one's family for days, and finally, asking the woman where she was from, where she was headed, and if she had company. The woman said that her name was Shantha. When she confirmed that she was travelling alone to Karnataka to meet her husband who worked in a mill there, Shankar offered her a lift in his truck. Shankar sounded convincing enough when he said that the bus she had been waiting for was not going to turn up anytime soon, and even if it did, it would be too crowded for a woman to get into.

As they got into the truck, Shankar realised that there were shops scattered about the place, and houses by the side of the road for the next few kilometres. It would, therefore, not be safe to attack the woman in an area where the struggle could be witnessed by someone manning one of the shops or dhabas, lazying in front of one of the houses, or strolling by the road. The woman had to be driven to a secluded place. Shankar kept talking to the woman, gaining her confidence, making her feel safe in his company. The womanly scent of her sweat-slick body fanned the fire in his loins.

Shantha felt uncomfortable for the first time when the conversation stopped and the truck took a diversion off the highway to the right. They trudged along a dusty, bumpy road. There were empty arid fields on both sides, and there was no trace of human habitation within miles.

By the time Shankar pulled up, Shantha realised that her worst apprehension had come true. She had been abducted, and there was virtually nothing that she could do about the situation. There was no way she would be able to overpower the burly man. Even if she cried her lungs out, there was no one to hear and come to her rescue.

Shankar stopped the engine and leapt out of the car. He opened the door next to the passenger seat and pulled Shantha out, like a rag doll.

When Shantha tried to scream, Shankar slapped her hard across her face and asked her to shut up. Her upper lip split and she felt the salty, metallic taste of blood oozing into her mouth. Her knees gave away and she collapsed on the ground. Shankar's face was now inches from hers – his long hair blowing in the wind, unbridled lust burning in his bloodshot eyes, his teeth bared under his thick moustache, the fire in his breath searing her skin. When she tried to scream again, Shankar gagged her with his towel, raining blows on her head and her abdomen. When she had lost all her power to fight the monster, he started tearing her clothes off.

***

When his hunger had been satiated, Shankar took a long, hard look at the woman. She was sprawled on the dust, naked, dead from the innumerable wounds inflicted by his machete. This was not new to him. However, this was the first time that he had violated and murdered a woman who did not peddle her body for money. He wondered why he had been fixated on the hookers all these days! Just any woman would be fine. As long as his act went undetected.

He remembered that he had often gone back to the sites, where he had dumped bodies, to take stock of the situation after several days. On several occasions, he had not found the bodies, barring probably a few bones here and there. The bodies had been ravaged by dogs, foxes, field mice, birds – a whole variety of them, feeding on the carcasses, cleaning up for him. It was therefore best to leave the disfigured body of the woman right there on the field. There was a whole bunch of beasts that would destroy the last shred of his victim.

Shankar put the machete back inside his bag and jumped into the driver's seat, feeling content.

Chapter 15

Before long, Shankar had come to realise that he could select *any* woman as a victim. People disappeared every day! It happened all the time. The public outrage invariably died down after a few days, and the police hit a dead-end after they had checked out the regular miscreants in the area, whose details they had in their files. That was also because in most cases, the bodies of the victims were not found, as they had been disposed off far from home, mutilated beyond recognition, eaten away by animals and birds.

Shankar started picking up women randomly from roads, farms and houses in the villages by the highways that he sneaked into when the women were alone. The fact that he could speak fluently in Tamil, Telugu, Kannada and Hindi came to his aid, as he could befriend and pick up women quite easily. He could easily engage his victims in conversation. He would chat and flatter and entertain, making the whole encounter seem legitimate and secure to start with.

"It's not easy driving around in trucks across four states when you have three lovely daughters at home. I miss them so much!"

"I keep worrying about my wife having to take care of the house and my three daughters while I am away! It must be so difficult for her."

"Why don't I give you a lift? You know, these roads are not safe for a beautiful woman like you."

"I feel so lonely driving for hours on these highways. I am lucky to have someone so jovial and smart like you travelling with me today."

"I've been driving all day and have run out of water. Thank god, I saw your house by the road. Would you be kind enough to offer me a glass of water, if that's not asking for too much?"

It was like acting out a role. In the early days, the friendly banter, in addition to putting the woman at ease, also helped Shankar to keep his own mind away in the initial stages of his interaction with the woman, from what he was going to do with her eventually. He knew that if he focused too much on the final act right from the beginning, then he would become edgy, lose his concentration, or somehow betray his evil intentions, which the woman might notice easily. However, over a period of time, Shankar did not have to try too hard. The more an actor plays a certain kind of role, the better he gets at it, and can do his job spontaneously.

Shankar kept getting better at his role – to charm and then harm.

PART THREE

COMPLACENCY KILLS

Chapter 16

3rd July 2009

Shyamala, a 45-year-old woman from Perandahalli, near Hosur in Tamil Nadu, was on her way to the market to buy groceries when the truck went past her, blowing a cloud of dust on her face. It was getting late, and she had to hurry. Her husband would be home soon, and she had to get the dinner ready in time.

The truck stopped abruptly a few feet ahead, and the driver stepped out, carrying a black bag. Shyamala's heart started beating fast when she saw the man walking towards her in long, brisk steps. The warm wind blowing over the fields around her moaned in her ears. The man was now within an arm's length.

"Where are you headed, all alone? It's late and the roads are not safe around here," Shankar slurred. His breath reeked of liquor.

Shyamala's heart drummed against her ribs. "I will be fine, thank you," she said as she tried to walk past the man who now stood in front of her, obstructing her way.

"I can drop you wherever you are going…" Shankar said. He tried to sound as convincing as the liquor would allow him to. But he knew right away that something was off.

"Thank you, I'll manage," Shyamala tried again to go around the beefy man who continued to block her way.

"Fucking bitch!" Shankar screamed. He did not realise what had come over him. He grabbed the woman by her neck and shoved her into a bush by the road. No preparation, no planning, no disguise, no smooth talk. Shankar allowed himself to be driven purely by impulse.

When Shyamala cried out for help, Shankar put a hand on her mouth and brandished the machete which he had pulled out of the bag in the meantime. "Shut up," he whispered menacingly in Shyamala's ears. He made a terrifying sight with his long hair ruffled by the wind, drool dripping off his moist lips, his lustful eyes devouring his prey, hands fumbling clumsily with her clothes. Shyamala kept screaming, and he kept telling her to be quiet. She flailed her arms and legs helplessly, aiming at his crotch but missing every time.

Shankar knew that there were houses not too far away. He was concerned that someone might hear the woman, but he had gone too far down the road now to retreat. The monster inside him had been aroused, and now it had to be satiated at any cost. He tried to silence her by choking her neck, even as he raised her saree past her thighs. All he wanted was to throttle her into unconsciousness so that she would stop screaming and he could have his way with her.

That was when he heard the noises behind him, rising above the muffled moans of the woman. Sitting on his knees between her legs, his hand still around her neck, Shankar turned around and saw the shadows running towards him. The over-excited, over-aroused and compulsive state of his mind gave way to panic in no time. Those must be men from the nearby houses who had heard the woman. He could not figure out how many of them were there, but he knew for sure that he would not be able to take on them, especially in his inebriated condition.

Shankar stood up on heavy legs, and picked up his bag, quickly stuffing the machete inside it. As he started running towards his truck, Shyamala grabbed a leg, still coughing and trying to catch her breath. Even as her nails dug into his flesh, Shankar gathered all the strength he could muster and freed himself, kicking her off his leg.

By the time the men reached the spot, Shankar had got into his truck and started the engine.

That evening, a case was filed in the local police station against the trucker who had tried to rape and murder P. Shyamala. The police interrogated Shyamala and noted down the description of the perpetrator.

Though Shankar had started his rampage in the previous year, this was the first time that a police case was formally lodged against him, and his appearance was documented.

A few weeks later, on 23rd August 2009, Shankar picked up Constable Priyamani from the Adhiyur Road junction. Her rape and murder triggered off the massive manhunt across four states.

Chapter 17

Shankar tossed and turned restlessly on his bed as sleep eluded him. He could hear the night-birds and the dogs, the occasional cars and trucks swooshing down the highway that was not very far from the empty shack by a farm where he had put up for the night. He sat up and picked up the empty bottle of country liquor from the floor. He brought the bottle to his mouth and turned it upside down, expecting a drop or two to wet his dry tongue.

But no luck! This was a bad night.

His mind was agitated over the events of the evening. It was the restlessness of a man who had left a job half-done.

***

Shankar saw the girl get off a van on the Salem highway. She seemed to be in her early twenties. The man behind the wheel was about to stick his head out and wave her goodbye, when Shankar's truck came to an abrupt halt behind the van, and he started honking impatiently. The man swore under his breath and drove off, leaving a cloud of smoke behind.

Shankar watched the girl for a few seconds, as she stepped off the highway into a road that went through an empty field.

He turned the engine off and leapt out of his truck, carrying his bag with the machete. He followed the girl down the dusty road. His eyes were fixed on her bottom all the time, shuffling under her salwar-kurta, fanning the fire that raged through his veins. He noticed that there were a few scattered houses on the other side of the field. One of those was probably where she was heading to. This was the time when he would have to make his move before she went any closer to the settlement.

He took the girl by surprise, pouncing on her from behind, placing his hand on her mouth and dragging her behind a bush by the road. He pinned the girl to the ground and got on top of her. Her muffled cries were buried in the din of birds flocking homewards as the setting sun painted the sky in hues of red and purple. Her unbelieving eyes seemed to pop out of her sockets, the veins on her forehead threatening to burst. The beast, straddling her, strangled her with one hand and began to undo the knot of her salwar with the other.

***

By the time Shankar emptied himself inside the girl, the cover of darkness had started spreading over the field. The limp body of the girl was sprawled under him. She had stopped struggling long back, and it appeared that she was unconscious. She was bleeding profusely. Shankar sat on his haunches contentedly and took in the spectacle for a few seconds. He then pulled the machete out of his bag.

As he got ready to strike the first blow, he heard a sound that he had least expected to hear.

A cycle bell!

He craned his neck and peeped above the bush. Sure enough! There was a man coming this way from the direction of the huts. The cycle was still quite far from where the girl was lying behind the bush, battered and bruised, the dry earth soaking in her blood. But Shankar was scared. He did not want to take a chance. He put the machete back inside his bag and stood up. Without looking back, he started walking briskly in the direction of the highway.

When he had almost reached the truck, he thought he heard the girl moaning.

The next moment, he dismissed the idea. He was way too far from the girl, and she was probably dead by now. It was probably the wind. It could be an animal that had crept out of its hole in the dark. It could even be his mind playing tricks with him.

The girl must be dead by now. She had to be.

***

It was past midnight, and Shankar's mind was still tense and agitated. Even the bottle of liquor had failed to put him to sleep. He kept thinking about the girl behind the bush. He should have hacked the bitch into pieces. What if she had not died? What if the man had found her? What if they had gone to the police by now?

He sat at the edge of his cot and kept thinking with his head buried in his hands. Finally, he decided.

There was no point sitting on his bum and speculating. He would return to the scene and find out for himself. There were only two possibilities, and he had nothing to lose either way. If the girl was dead and the body was still there, then he would pick up the corpse, along with her clothes, and dispose everything somewhere far from the village, where there was no chance of anyone finding her. If the body was not there, then there was a chance, however remote, that the girl was alive, and he would drive off that very night to some place far away and lie low for a few days.

Shankar got dressed and climbed onto his truck.

***

When Shankar reached the scene, he turned off the engine of his truck and remained seated for a while, looking out of the window at the fields, trying to figure out, in his confused state of mind, where exactly he had fucked the bitch and left her to die. He could not see anyone in the vicinity and felt somewhat relieved. Had the bitch been found, would the place not be teeming with policemen by now? Would the people in the village not have flocked around the spot?

None of that had happened. He was now certain that he would find the body in the same place, in the same position as he had left it. The dogs and the rats might have feasted on bits and pieces of her. Driving down here was, after all, a good idea. He would pick the corpse up, dump it somewhere convenient, and then sleep the rest of the night off in his truck.

Shankar walked down the path along which he had followed the girl a few hours back. The breeze felt nice on his face and the silence all around calmed his turbulent mind. Running his fingers through his hair, he walked around the bush, relishing the thought of finding the corpse – cold and stiff, soaked in blood, eaten away here and there – but still there. At that moment, there was nothing more important to him.

But the body was not there!

At first, Shankar could not believe his eyes. He must have had too much of the hooch. He rubbed his eyes and looked again. He was disappointed once again. The next moment, he thought that he must have come to the wrong place. It was dark, he was drunk, and his mind had been acting up since the evening. That had to be the wrong bush.

As he was about to turn, the lights came up!

Shankar stood like a deer caught in headlights – the police flashlights, to be precise. He stood rooted to the ground that was still tainted by the blood of the girl he had raped in the evening. He raised an arm to shield his eyes from the glare, still unable to make sense of what was going on.

It all made sense, finally, when through the blinding haze, he saw three guns aimed at him.

"Don't move or we'll shoot!"

Chapter 18

19th October 2009

Swaminathan picked up the phone after the first ring.

It had been a month since the body of Constable Priyamani had been discovered and the very thought that her killer was still roaming free, despite the best efforts of the investigation team, irked him. Reports of bodies of women – raped, murdered and mutilated – turning up in empty fields and graveyards along the highways in Tirupur, Salem and Dharmapuri areas had been flowing in. It was as if the killer had thrown a challenge at the police machinery, and Swaminathan had led his team into a wild goose chase, that had not gone anywhere so far.

In July, the Perandahalli police station had received a complaint from a woman named P. Shyamala about a trucker who had intercepted her while she had been on her way to the grocery store and had tried to rape and strangle her. The police had a description of the man, which they had shared with Swaminathan. He, in turn, had passed it on to all the police stations in the area. Swaminathan was sure that was the man they had all been looking for all these days. He was confident that it was a matter of time before he would be caught.

Swaminathan had spent the last month almost entirely in his office, coordinating activities of his team spread out across the states, taking calls from police stations along the highways, visiting crime scenes, listening to reports from teams – those who were stationed at the state borders to check vehicles travelling up and down, or those that patrolled the villages along the highways.

Swaminathan had worked for years in that office. The office had one small window, but he observed the world from there. In that ten-feet-square office, he had learned the tricks of his trade, celebrated his victories, cried in defeat, and acquired the insights he now had into the criminal mind. He had been banking heavily on his experience over the last one month.

He had not spared time for his family. He had not had a good night's sleep in all these weeks. He did not remember the last time he had eaten a full meal. As he led his army from the front, the dark circles under his eyes, the dishevelled hair and the growing stubble, and his visibly deteriorating health further egged on his soldiers. He jumped up and grabbed the receiver every time the phone rang on his desk. That day was no exception.

The call was from Salem.

A girl in her twenties was raped by the monster the previous evening and left to die on a field near Salem highway, next to a road that went to her village. A passer-by found her, brought her back to the village, and the girl reported to the local police. Night patrol was deployed in the area. Armed policemen were scattered around the place, hiding behind bushes, their eyes on the road that stretched from the highway to the village, with the expectation that the killer might return to take stock of his unfinished job. A man did turn up in a truck after midnight. He started checking behind the bushes by the road, where the rape had been committed. The guards found his movements suspicious and converged on him from three sides. When he was apprehended and brought to the police station, it was found that he matched not only the description of the rapist as stated by the victim, but also the description which had been shared by Swaminathan earlier from the incident at Perandahalli near Hosur. That was, beyond any reasonable doubt, the man whom the task force had been looking for.

As Swaminathan listened, his lips curved into a smile, and his eyes welled up.

On the same day, M. Jaishankar was arrested by Tirupur police. The reign of terror on the highways was finally over. The devil had finally been caught!

Chapter 19

Swaminathan stood outside the police station at Coimbatore, and lighted the first cigarette of the day. He looked up at the sky. The soft warmth of the October morning sun felt soothing. He had finally slept through the night before. A deep, uninterrupted, dreamless sleep. A few days back, that had seemed impossible. Swaminathan inhaled the smoke deep into his lungs and felt the mixture of nicotine and fresh air charge up his system.

He looked at his watch. He wanted to be on time for the meeting with the Coimbatore City Police Commissioner, C. Raghavendra Babu. Shankar had been transferred to the Coimbatore Central Jail, and as the police got ready for the trial, they wanted to make sure that they had a sound understanding of the way Shankar's mind worked. The commissioner had expressed his desire to have a detailed discussion with Swaminathan to better understand the method behind Shankar's madness. He had also invited eminent psychologist Dr S. Ramanathan for the meeting.

When Swaminathan stepped into the room, he saw that the commissioner and the psychologist had already taken their seats. They stood up as soon as Swaminathan entered the room. The commissioner extended his hand and said, "Congratulations, Swami! This is a landmark achievement. I know how hard you and your team have worked over the last several weeks. Sleepless nights, personal sacrifices, failing health – but at the end of it all, everything seems worthwhile today."

"Thank you, sir," Swaminathan said as he shook the commissioner's hand. As they took their seats, Swaminathan said, "It was surprisingly not very difficult to get him to confess to all the crimes! We have twenty cases of rape registered against him so far, of which he also murdered the victims in thirteen cases. I have a feeling that the numbers could be much more. In fact, hearing him narrate the incidents, it seemed to me as if he was rather proud of what he had done. If there was any remorse, I thought it came from the fact that he had been caught, not because of what he had been doing."

The commissioner nodded and turned towards the psychologist. He said, "That is the reason why we wanted to discuss this case with you, Doctor. This knowledge would be important for us during the trial."

Dr Ramanathan cleared his throat and said, "Commissioner, I must thank you for sharing with me the details of this case. I think this man is a classic example of how a serial killer usually functions. You see, every time a serial murderer kills, the person typically goes through a mental process involving six stages.

"The first is called the 'aura' stage, where the person starts losing the grip on reality. The killer gets detached from the real world and finds himself in a virtual world conjured up by his twisted mind. To cut a long story short, the actual act of killing is the fifth stage, which is called the 'totem' stage. You can think of this stage as the climax. For the killer, however, it is an anti-climactic stage, as the killer, after a momentary phase of contentment, is always unable to fulfil the expectations of satisfaction and catharsis, which the person had had from the act of killing. So, the killer goes to the sixth stage which is the 'depressed' stage. This in turn eventually leads the killer to a new aura stage, getting ready for the next killing. However, as the killer goes through this never-ending cycle, the killer's behaviour changes over the long term. With time, you start seeing a decreased level of control and an increased level of brutality.

"The first time a person kills, the time taken to recover from the aftershock is longer. The so-called 'cooling down' period is the longest. It leads to a long aura phase, where the killer takes time to prepare and plan for the next killing. I am quite sure that if you arrange the murders committed by Shankar chronologically, you will find that the longest cool-off period was after his first killing."

"You are right, Doctor," said Swaminathan. "His first victim was a prostitute. He lay low for several weeks after that first murder."

Dr Ramanathan nodded and said, “This is a common pattern. If the killer takes a lot of care about the details in the crime scene, and if the chances of discovery are little, it suggests that the killer is still in the early days. In this phase, one is trying to perfect one’s technique, almost like an art, and to become more efficient. This is the most difficult phase to catch the killer.

“However, after the killer has succeeded a few times, you start observing a change. The cool-off periods become shorter and shorter. There is not enough planning, the murders are almost like acts of impulse. The killer is prone to take greater risks.”

“This is true for Shankar! Towards the end, he had been acting on impulse. Take the case of Shyamala in Hosur, for example. Or the incident in Salem, which led to his arrest,” said the commissioner.

Dr Ramanathan smiled and said, “The examples do support the theory! Incidentally, the killer also gets more brutal with time. This indicates that the killer’s frustration is growing. The killer’s thirst for blood is on the rise, and satisfaction from the killings is on the decline.”

“Shankar had certainly reached that point! In September this year, he killed a fifty-year-old woman in Namakkal at her farm. He hacked the woman with a sickle and severed one of her limbs. He raped her and robbed her of a gold chain!” Swaminathan said.

"This is the point at which the killer loses self-control and is easier to catch," said Dr Ramanathan, "This is where you got lucky, since Shankar apparently had lived through all these phases, and had become reckless with his frustration and insatiable hunger."

There was silence in the room for some time. Then, the commissioner spoke.

"What about justification? Does a serial killer like Shankar justify these brutal killings? I mean, what kind of justification can be built in for killing another helpless human being? For one's own enjoyment? That's what it amounts to at the end of the day, doesn't it?"

Dr Ramanathan said, "Justification is an interesting topic. Forget about the serial killer for a minute. In our urban society, we have one person killing another with the justification *'he would have killed me if I didn't kill him'*. A terrorist committing mass murder may say, *'I am serving a greater cause, for which these people had to be sacrificed. Among the millions of people in the world, a dozen men and women would not be missed, in any case. So what, if there are a dozen human beings lesser on the face of the planet? What difference will it make a hundred years from now?'* Again, it is a common excuse on the part of molesters and rapists that the victim lured them on, or were trying to excite or arouse them through her actions or by the way she dressed. Unfortunately, we even have political leaders who endorse that justification.

"As you can see, these are not justifications at all! These are attempts made by these persons to *cope with their need to kill or rape or abuse*. Instead of coping with what is really driving them to commit the crime, they are trying to come up with these so-called justifications.

"Let us now turn to Shankar's case. Shankar would never accept the fact that he is sick and extremely weak. The rest of us can clearly see there is something seriously wrong with the way his mind works. We know, what he has done is not reasonable or logical or justifiable. However, *he* doesn't realise this. *He* doesn't think rationally. Had he been rational, then he would have tried to figure out the cause of the problem himself or sought someone else's help. If he could really look inwards, he would have identified what it was that made him think and act the way he did. If he could identify, isolate and control those aspects of his personality, then he would probably not have engaged in that kind of behaviour. Instead, he felt that he had to satisfy his need by raping and killing – one woman after another. *That was his justification for himself*. But that didn't address the problem. He became just a ticking time bomb, waiting for the next opportunity to explode. As in all the other examples I mentioned just now, Shankar was trying to cope with the need, rather than deal with what caused that need."

"You mentioned an expectation of satisfaction and contentment from these killings. What did Shankar really expect from these deaths? Why did he go down this path at all? I asked him the same question. He could not answer," Swaminathan said.

Dr Ramanathan looked at Swaminathan for a few seconds and asked, "Tell me Inspector, do you watch cricket?"

"I do," Swaminathan replied promptly.

"On the face of it, someone could call a game of cricket really stupid! A pair of batsmen hitting a ball all around the park and eleven men running after it. But *why* do people still love watching the game? We don't have an answer. It's the same with Shankar. It must have been equally difficult for him to answer your question!

"I think in the beginning, it was probably not his goal to *kill* his victims. It was about his *possession* of something or someone desirable. Someone brought up in a different environment might take to stealing cars, for example. In Shankar's case, it was *women* – in itself, an anti-social idea. Shankar then found out that he loved to torture his victims as he violated them."

"Yes, he did confess that he loved beating up the women," Swaminathan interjected.

"His need to gratify his urge, in some cases, led to the deaths of these victims. There is another way of looking at this. He might have felt that taking the life of his victim was the ultimate form of possession. However, I think that in most cases, the idea of killing the victim came from his need to eliminate the witness of his crime – the victim herself, and make sure that the crime went undetected."

The ACP turned to Swaminathan and said, "You mentioned a possibility that Shankar had killed more women, who had not been discovered. What makes you think so?"

"Looking at his modus operandi, sir," Swaminathan said. "For all the freedom and mobility that he enjoyed, I feel this is a distinct possibility. For every death that was publicised, there could be one that was not. Hundreds of women are reported missing in these states every day and are never heard of again!"

The discussion continued for some more time, as the three men found themselves traversing the labyrinthine tracks that led to the darkest recesses of the twisted mind of one of the most notorious killers the world had ever seen.

Chapter 20

When twenty-five-year-old M. Kondasamy received the order, it took him a while to process what he had just been told. A variety of emotions erupted in his mind.

He was proud and happy that he had been considered worthy of carrying out what was undoubtedly a critical and high-risk assignment. Kondasamy came from Irumattur, a small village in Harur taluk. He had joined the force only three years back. After serving in the Seventh Battalion of the Tamil Nadu Special Police, he had been deployed in the Coimbatore City Police Armed Reserve Force in December last year. To be entrusted with the responsibility of escorting notorious serial killer M. Jaishankar for three consecutive days was a big deal. It was surely going to be an experience of a lifetime – the kind of story he could tell his grandchildren, in the later years of his life.

At the same time, Kondasamy was aware of the fact that it was not going to be easy. The man was nothing short of a merciless monster. Everyone in the force had, by that time, come to know about the brutal rapes and murders the man had been charged with. Apparently, he had raped twenty women, and killed more than a dozen of them! Having to escort him across three courts called for a heightened sense of responsibility, alertness and courage.

Shankar had to be produced in the Namakkal court on Wednesday, 16th of March, in Tiruchirappalli the following day, and finally in Dharmapuri on Friday, 18th of March. He would have to be brought back to the prison in Coimbatore from Dharmapuri.

Kondasamy was happy that joining him in his mission would be Rajaram, with whom he shared a rented house near the Armed Reserve Police grounds. They were thick friends, and Kondasamy was confident that together, they would manage to pull it off, however difficult the task seemed.

***

18th March 2011

It was nine in the night when Kondasamy and Rajaram arrived at Salem Bus Depot, about a hundred and thirty kilometres from their destination in Coimbatore, along with Shankar.

Kondasamy was relieved that the arduous three days had finally ended. As if keeping an eye on the deadly killer was not enough, Rajaram and he had had to handle the media persons and crowds of onlookers everywhere they had gone. The killer had surprisingly not been as difficult to handle as Kondasamy had imagined. In fact, on certain occasions, Kondasamy had the feeling that the maniac was enjoying the attention of the media, and the curiosity of the people who thronged the roads near the courts. They jostled each other to catch a glimpse of the man who had spread havoc in those towns.

Thankfully, all of that was now coming to an end. It was now a matter of a few hours. Kondasamy silently congratulated himself on a job well done.

Kondasamy looked at Shankar and thought that the bastard must be missing the public attention at that moment. The police were not allowed to handcuff criminals when they were being transported in public areas. Shankar, therefore, did not stand out from the crowd in the bus depot. He was just another face in the crowd, one of the hundreds of busy men and women running in every direction in the bus depot late in the evening, hoping to board a bus that would take them home, away on a holiday, or back to work.

That, however, did not deter Shankar from demanding the celebrity treatment that he had been getting used to. “Let me tell you, I am not going to travel in one of those state transport buses, in case that’s what you guys have in mind,” Shankar smirked at Rajaram. “All my life, I have travelled alone in my truck on empty highways. I am not used to crowds. They make me sick. Now that isn’t something we want, do we? Let’s find out when the next Super Deluxe leaves.”

Kondasamy and Rajaram exchanged glances. There was no point arguing. Rajaram went away to find a timetable for super deluxe buses and get three tickets for the next available bus.

Shankar yawned and stretched his arms.

"I think a cup of masala chai before we board the bus won't be a bad idea, what do you say?" he turned towards Kondasamy and asked. "Isn't that a tea-stall out there?" Shankar pointed his finger to the left. Kondasamy turned in the direction Shankar had pointed at and squinted his eyes. There indeed was a tea-stall at the far end of the depot. He could do with a cup of sweet tea himself. It had been a long day at the Dharmapuri fast-track court. The heat did not help. There were large patches of sweat on his shirt, and he felt completely drained of energy. "Let's wait for Rajaram to return and we can—" he said as he turned towards Shankar.

As he looked to his right, his heart sank. For a few seconds, he felt like he had been paralysed.

Shankar was not there!

He looked all around himself, there was no trace of the man. It seemed as if he had vanished in the air like a wisp of smoke, making it look so incredibly easy! Kondasamy kept looking helplessly at the faces of unknown men and women who went past him in all directions, but there was no sign of that one face that he longed more than anything else to see at that moment.

When Rajaram returned with the tickets, they decided to go in different directions. They looked in the toilets. They looked inside buses, packed and empty. They asked around and gave descriptions to check if anyone had seen Shankar. The two constables ran around, inside the depot and then outside, like men possessed, making their way through thick crowds, shoving people down with no time for an apology, trying to cover maximum ground in the shortest possible time, pushed harder and harder by the knowledge that with every passing minute, the killer was running further and further away from the law. They wished they could make time stand still. After all these days, all it took was a moment's distraction to lose the most wanted man of the state in a crowded bus depot!

When three hours had passed, Rajaram made a call to Coimbatore and informed the officials there. The police in Coimbatore, in turn, informed their counterparts in Salem.

Rajaram and Kondasamy boarded a bus to return to Coimbatore.

***

As Kondasamy looked out of the window, the wind ruffling his hair, the tears finally broke free. The world around him was a blur. He wiped his tears off with his shirt sleeve, but they were back again. He had failed in his duty, and failed miserably. The serial killer was now free, and he was the only one to blame. It was he, and no one else, who had slipped.

Overwhelmed by his remorse, Kondasamy also wondered what the future had in store for him. He was sure that his negligence would not be excused at any cost. There was no doubt that the harshest of punishments awaited him at Coimbatore. His fate was sealed. There would be no stories for his grandchildren.

Kondasamy did not notice when the bus had stopped at the Bharathiyar Road bus stop at Pappanaickenpalayam. Rajaram patted him on the back and said, "Get up! We're getting down here." Kondasamy got up on rubbery legs, his head spinning, and followed Rajaram out of the bus.

"Kondasamy, you need to get a grip on yourself! We'll explain everything to the bosses, and I'm sure they'll understand. Don't forget that the bastard had fooled the entire police force for more than a year before he was caught. He is a cunning sonofabitch—" Rajaram kept talking to his friend who walked wearily behind him. They were near the rear gate of the Police Recruits School.

Rajaram stopped in his tracks when he heard the gunshot.

When he slowly turned around, he saw Kondasamy lying on the road in a heap, the pool of blood widening around his still body. Kondasamy had shot himself in the chin, the bullet making an exit through the left side of his skull. Rajaram let out a guttural scream and fell on his knees. Before everything turned black, he saw a courier boy running towards them, windows opening in the houses around him and people running out on the street.

***

M. Jaishankar, the terror of the highways, was on the loose.

PART FOUR

THE FUGITIVE

Chapter 21

The Coimbatore police got into action immediately. The monster was on the loose and had to be brought back as soon as possible.

A special team was put together under Police Inspector (Crime), Coimbatore Police, P Muthuswamy. The first thing Muthuswamy did was to get in touch with Swaminathan. "No one understands the beast better than you do," he said. "I will request your support in leading the task force." Swaminathan did not refuse. He wanted to see Shankar back behind bars as badly as anyone in the Coimbatore police force.

Muthuswamy put together a task force comprising of fifteen police personnel, with two sub-inspectors reporting to him. In the first meeting of the task force, Swaminathan explained to everyone in the room, the modus operandi Shankar had followed as he had spread havoc along the highways in Tirupur, Salem and Dharmapuri districts. He would pick up prostitutes, and target women in farms and in their houses in villages by the roads. He would rape them and torture them brutally, sometimes robbing them of their precious belongings, and eventually killing them. He would then dump their mutilated bodies in empty fields or graveyards, far from where these women came from. The bodies would be ravaged by animals and would not be found easily. Even when they were found, the police would take time to connect the discovery of the disfigured body of a woman to a missing person report in a different area. By that time, Shankar would have moved on to his next victim.

"Where do you think he would go after escaping from the police?" Muthuswamy asked.

Swaminathan thought for a while and said, "He knows that right after his escape from Salem, the police across the state would be on high alert. My guess is that he would try to escape from Tamil Nadu. He would run away to a neighbouring state – Karnataka, Andhra Pradesh, Kerala." He paused briefly, and then said, "He would lie low for a few days, and then, I am afraid, he will start again. I would suggest we alert the police in these states as well."

There was silence in the room. It took time for the ominous words of Swaminathan to sink in.

"We have all been fearing the worst, Inspector, right from the day Shankar escaped from that bus depot in Salem. But let us take a step back and ask ourselves how real and how justified our fear is. What makes you think that Shankar will go back to his old ways, after all that he has gone through since his arrest in 2009?" Muthuswamy asked.

Swaminathan smiled and said, "With all due respect for the manner in which we run our jails, there is nothing in our prisons of a therapeutic nature that would have made

Shankar a reformed man with a change in his habits. If the type of person he is – a psychopath who has raped and murdered numerous women – was back on the roads after a long period of incarceration, we can assume with a high degree of confidence that he will go back to his old ways once again. I do not believe that he has received anything inside our jails that might have helped him sort out his sickness."

Muthuswamy realised why Swaminathan was famous for calling a spade a spade.

"But would he not still be afraid of being caught? In fact, more than he had been before? He knows now that the police know him, his face is known to the public, he has already been convicted in a series of cases, and there is bound to be a manhunt across the four states? Isn't it therefore more likely that he would withdraw into a cave and stay in hiding?" Muthuswamy asked.

"I will disagree," said Swaminathan. "You see, he is fresh out of jail. To your point, he does have a horror about being in prison. No one, who has not been in jail on a serious charge for several months, can even imagine how hard it is. Especially, for the first few months. But here is the catch! For anyone who has survived those first six months, the idea of being in a jail begins to lose its impact. The person gets used to jail. Being jailed is no more a horrific idea! That is the reason why we see so many people going back to a life of crime after they have served a sentence and have been released. I hope there will be a day when our criminal justice system realises this hard truth. If you keep a man in jail beyond a certain period of time, he learns to adapt to prison, he learns how to satisfy most of his needs in jail, he builds his network of friends, and then imprisonment loses all its significance. A long incarceration numbs out the sensitivities of an individual, so much so that when he is back on the streets again, he is less fearful of prison, and hence, more inclined to criminal behaviour. Jail is no longer that unknown, threatening, horrible place he was once so afraid of! As for the common man knowing how he looks, you know as well as I do what a clean shave and a haircut can do to alter a man's face!"

The harsh truth stared everyone in the face, as Muthuswamy ended the meeting after thanking Swaminathan.

When everyone was about to leave the conference room, an official came running inside. He went to Muthuswamy and said, "Sir, Shankar's phone has been activated. He is in Bellary."

"Connect me to Bellary, right away!" Muthuswamy smiled and looked triumphantly at Swaminathan, who stood next to him, "You were right! The bastard has sneaked off to Karnataka!"

"Strange!" Swaminathan muttered, as he wrinkled his brows.

Chapter 22

"What makes you think that it's strange that Shankar is using his mobile phone?" asked Muthuswamy.

Swaminathan took a drag of his cigarette and said, "We found out that Shankar had stopped using his mobile phone after the rape and murder of Priyamani, the lady constable, in 2009. That was when he realised that the police would be hot on his trail. It is surprising that after all these years, when he has escaped from the police and is on the run, he has started using his phone! Don't you find that strange?"

Muthuswamy smiled and said, "Or maybe he's taking it easy! The escape has made him complacent. Who knows?"

Swaminathan muttered to himself, "Very unlike him, I must say." He then looked at Muthuswamy and asked, "Who is he calling, by the way?"

"Mostly his family. We are going to pay them a visit."

"That's even stranger!" said Swaminathan.

***

Sub-Inspector Sivaraman walked through an alleyway where the houses stood cheek by jowl and the pavement served as extensions of their drawing rooms, where people were reading newspapers, listening to transistors, cooking or taking an afternoon nap. A few little girls looked at him wide-eyed. The more courageous ones giggled at him. He asked a woman sitting behind a sewing machine, and she showed him the door he was looking for.

Rajeshwari was not particularly happy on seeing the police at her doorstep.

Sivaraman looked around the single-room house with its old furniture, broken windows, dirty curtains, and a creaking bed with a soiled mattress barely covered by a sheet with gaping holes. A narrow corridor outside the room doubled up as kitchen. Rajeshwari was busy cleaning utensils, one of her daughters helping her. Another daughter sat on her haunches next to her mother and was cutting vegetables, occasionally stealing glances at the uniformed policeman, whose bulky frame seemed to fill up the entire room. The third daughter, the youngest, sat on the bed with a book open in front of her, but had her eyes fixed on Sivaraman's holster, and her mouth open in innocent wonder.

"When was the last time you saw Jaishankar?" Sivaraman asked.

Rajeshwari dropped the aluminium plate she was cleaning with a clang and looked at Sivaraman. "More than three years back," she said. "That man left us – me and our three daughters. He never came back. He never sent us any money and he stopped calling us. He didn't bother to find out how his daughters were. It would have made no difference to him, even if they had died of hunger. I have been doing odd jobs for the last three years to feed my daughters and to pay the fees for their school. I would have to get the eldest married off in a few years!" Her eyes welled up as she spoke, the pain and anger that she had kept buried in the hidden chambers of her heart threatening to burst out in the deluge of tears.

"Then we came to know what he had been up to," she looked at her daughters and lowered her voice. "He brought disgrace to the family. The neighbours stopped visiting us. They would shut their windows on our faces. They would not let their children talk to my daughters or play with them. Some of them even suggested that he had left home and taken to raping women, as I had not been able to satisfy him in bed!"

"I understand what you have gone through—" Sivaraman began in a conciliatory tone, but was not allowed to finish.

"No, you don't! You have no idea," Rajeshwari lashed out, "and now you are here to harass me. That is all that the police is good for!"

"I do not intend to bother you. I need some information. You do know that he escaped from the police a few days back, don't you?" asked Sivaraman.

Rajeshwari nodded.

"Has he been calling you?"

"Yes, he called me a few times after all these years," said Rajeshwari after a moment's hesitation. "I was surprised. In fact, I told him to stop calling me, as I don't want to talk to him!"

"What did he say?"

"Nothing that would be of interest to the police. Was asking after the daughters, about my work – you know, the usual drill."

"Did he say where he is, or where he is planning to go?"

"No, he didn't say any of that and I didn't ask as I don't care. It is your job to find that out, isn't it?"

The youngest girl ran to her mother, and casting a cautious glance at Sivaraman, asked, "Amma, is the policeman going to arrest appa?" Rajeshwari hugged her tight, without answering her question.

Sivaraman stood up. He walked up to the girl and placed his hand on her head, smiling. He did not, however, have any words to placate her. He asked Rajeshwari for a piece of paper and scribbled his phone number on it. Handing it over to her, he said, "If you hear anything about his whereabouts or his plans, or if you need any help, call me."

He took one final look around the room and its occupants and walked out with a heavy heart.

Chapter 23

It was not long before the reports, which everyone had been apprehensive about, started flowing in. Gruesome incidents of rape and murder were on the rise in the Bellary, Tumkur and Chitradurga districts of Karnataka, mostly in farms along the highways, each bearing a striking resemblance with the killings in Tamil Nadu.

28th March 2011

Three women were raped and murdered in *a single day* in Nelahal village in Tumkur district.

31st March 2011

It was a warm and sultry summer afternoon in the Yaradakatte village in Tumkur district. Geetha and her husband Prashanth had finished lunch a while back. Geetha was busy cleaning utensils with the water she had drawn from the well in a pail. She was engrossed in her work, humming a tune, when her womanly instinct told her that she was being watched. She stopped scrubbing the aluminium vessel which had been gifted to her by her parents, along with other utensils, sarees and jewellery, when she had got married last year. She looked around, but did not see anyone. She noticed a stirring in the bushes bordering the farm behind her. Must be one of the dogs that turned up for leftovers after lunch and dinner. By some magic, the animals always managed to keep track of the time. She stood up and walked towards the bush, carrying leftovers in an aluminium thali.

She was a couple of feet away from the edge of the farm when the man jumped out and charged towards her like a bull. In no time, his muscular arms were around her. When Geetha had managed to recover from her initial shock, she started screaming for help. That, however, did not deter the man. He tried to shut her up by bringing his mouth down on hers, even as Geetha clawed his face, trying to free herself.

The man did not stop even when Prashanth stepped out of the hut on hearing the ruckus. Prashanth saw his wife squirming on the grass under a man who had pinned her down with his weight. "Let her go!" Prashanth cried out and picked up the stick that he used to drive animals away from the farm. The man looked up and rubbed the drool off his mouth with the back of his hand. He got off the woman and ran towards Prashanth. The man dealt a pile-driving punch into Prashanth's abdomen, and he doubled up in pain. The stick dropped to the floor. Even before Prashanth had caught his breath, the man hit him again, this time on his chest. The man kept showering blows on the hapless farmer. When Prasanth fell to the ground, the man dragged him back inside the hut and kept kicking him in the ribs till he fainted. Then, the man picked up the stick and stepped out of the hut.

He reached into his pocket and pulled out a matchbox. With his eyes fixed on Geetha, who had frozen with horror and the realisation of the impending doom, the man lit a couple of matchsticks and threw them casually on Prashanth's body, which lay on the floor face down. The brutality which Geetha had just seen with her own eyes was beyond her wildest imagination, and it had rendered her speechless. The man closed the door of the hut behind him, leaving the farmer to burn inside. By the time the man pounced on Geetha, she had passed out. In no time, the man started tearing her clothes off.

While the monster had his wife out in the open, at some point during the ghastly spectacle, Prashanth came back to his senses and his screams rent the air. The fire by that time had spread across the hut. The man, still moving in and out of the unconscious woman beneath him, turned towards the hut and smiled. "Serves the poor bugger right!" he muttered to himself.

After he had come inside the woman for the second time, the man stood up on rubbery legs and lowered his veshti. He walked towards the burning hut. He stooped to pick the stick up from the ground, his eyes fixed on the naked body a few feet away, which he had just ravaged. Clutching the stick firmly in his hand, the man went back to his victim. He raised the stick above his head, and it came down on the woman's skull at lightning speed.

The man did not stop till Geetha's face was a pulpy mess of blood, flesh and bones.

4th April 2011

A woman was raped and murdered in Tammenahalli village of Molakalmuru taluk in Chitradurga district. Another woman was raped and killed in Guilal village of Hiriyur taluk in Chitradurga district.

27th April 2011

A woman was raped, and her husband murdered in Seebar village of Chitradurga district.

Other than these incidents, by the end of April, the police had confirmed reports that Shankar had raped and killed six women in the Bellary district in Karnataka and killed two persons, including a child, in the Dharmapuri district in Tamil Nadu.

The summer of horror seemed to be never-ending.

***

The police were at a loss, as Shankar kept changing his locations. Around four thousand posters were put up at dhabas and highways, calling for a reward to anyone who provided any information about the elusive killer.

As Shankar kept using his phone to talk to his family in Salem, the location data collected since the time he had absconded suggested that he had moved from Salem to

Bellary, to other areas in the interiors of Karnataka, and then to Bangalore. The trajectory aligned with the places from where horrific crimes were being frequently reported. When the special team from Coimbatore arrived in Bangalore and joined the local police to hunt him down, they found no trace of Shankar. He also stopped making calls to his wife, having got wind that the police were fast catching up with him.

The next time the police managed to track his location, Shankar was in New Delhi!

Swaminathan could not put his finger on it, but something did not add up.

Chapter 24

28th April 2011

As Shankar turned the pages of the newspaper, his eyes got stuck on a report.

> *A notorious killer from Salem, who had escaped from police custody on 18th March by giving the slip to two constables escorting him from a fast-track court in Dharmapuri back to the prison in Coimbatore, had, in the intervening time, raped and killed six women in the Bellary district in Karnataka, and had murdered two persons in the Dharmapuri district in Tamil Nadu. The Coimbatore Police Commissioner C. Raghavendra Babu told reporters that the police had specific information about the crimes in Bellary and Dharmapuri. The police suspect that Shankar had been involved in other crimes in the Tumkur and Chitradurga districts in Karnataka. A special team had gone to Bangalore to nab him, but he had escaped to New Delhi. There is now a nation-wide manhunt for one of the most*

> *notorious killers the country has ever known of. Members of the task force have already travelled to New Delhi and are working with the local police to find the fugitive. Inspector P. Muthuswamy, who is leading the special team along with Inspector S. Swaminathan, who had arrested Jaishankar the last time, are confident that Shankar would soon be behind bars.*

Shankar smiled.

Over the last few weeks, he had made it a point to read the paper and watch the news on TV, whenever possible, to keep a tab on the investigation. Shankar read the accounts of the theories and speculations of the police with a critical eye. That helped put him in a far more advantageous position in comparison with the police. He knew when the police were right. He knew where the police were going wrong.

In the process, he had come to realise that the police and the media publicised a lot of information about an investigation, which should otherwise be kept hidden, from the perpetrator's perspective. The police, through the media, made speculations and arrived at conclusions in advance that often made Shankar laugh.

'... *he had escaped to New Delhi'* – yes, right!

Chapter 25

Muthuswamy and Swaminathan sat on a low wall outside the Police Headquarters watching the sun go down. Swaminathan took a long drag of his cigarette. Muthuswamy was a social smoker. He had picked up a stick from Swaminathan's pack, 'just to give him company'.

They had come to know a while back that Shankar had now moved to Mumbai from New Delhi.

"This makes no sense!" Muthuswamy looked agitated. "On the one hand, we have rapes and murders being reported from Karnataka, that look strikingly similar to Shankar's earlier crimes. Yet, his location data reveals that he was in New Delhi and now, in Mumbai. How is this even possible?"

Swaminathan did not speak for a while. Then, he blew out a cloud of smoke and stamped on the remainder of the cigarette stick under his boot. He turned towards Muthuswamy and smiled. He said, "This is one of the many things which have been bothering me lately. But I think I finally have the answers. Let us start from the start."

Muthuswamy nodded. "I found it strange that Shankar had started using his mobile phone again. As I told you, he had stopped using his phone when he had realised that the police would be after him, right after the body of the lady constable had been found in Tirupur in September 2009. So, why did he start using his phone after all these years? When we spoke to his wife, she confirmed our understanding that Shankar had not called her all these years. It was only after his escape from the bus depot at Salem that he had started calling her. Why?

"There can be only one answer. *Shankar wanted us to track his location through his mobile phone!*"

"Why would he want us to track his location when he is on the run?" Muthuswamy looked confused.

"So that we land up in the situation where we find ourselves today. We are struggling to figure out how he can be in two places at the same time! This is exactly what Shankar wanted," Swaminathan said, contemplating the cigarette smoke spiralling into the air.

"And you are saying, you have the answer to the riddle?" Muthuswamy sounded impatient. Swaminathan took his time lighting another cigarette and blowing out a mouthful of smoke. He seemed to be relishing his partner's anxiety. With a broad smile on his face, Swaminathan patted Muthuswamy on the back and said, "I do have the answer, Muthu. It lies not in call records and forensics reports, but in the criminal's wicked mind. And the simple answer is, *Shankar is not carrying his phone.*"

"What do you mean?" asked Muthuswamy.

"Why do you think Shankar stopped calling his wife after the special team had followed him to Bangalore, although his phone was active? That's because, he disposed of his mobile phone after he had reached Bangalore. *He left his mobile phone in a truck that went from Bangalore to New Delhi, and then to Mumbai.* He carried on with his heinous acts in Karnataka, while we kept looking for him elsewhere."

Muthuswamy's jaw dropped. He took a few seconds to process what he had just heard. Then he asked, "So what do you suggest we do now?"

"Very simple," Swaminathan said with a glint in his eyes, "we will beat him at his own game."

"How?" asked Muthuswamy.

"You see, thanks to the extensive media coverage of this investigation, every piece of information that we gather and every strategy that we make get publicised in no time. However, there is no point in blaming ourselves for sharing information with the media. Even if we do not speak to the media, in today's connected world, journalists will use their own sources and dig out reasonably accurate information in no time.

"For instance, only a couple of days back, the media screamed from the rooftops that we had tracked Shankar to New Delhi, and that a special team had been sent to work with the local police to catch him. What we don't realise is that the fugitive is also reading the newspaper, he is also watching the news bulletin on TV. He is always aware of how much we know and what we are planning to do next. This makes him alert and helps him plan his next step.

"In this case, if Shankar was going around killing women in Karnataka, and he was reading in the newspapers that we were looking for him in Delhi, he must have laughed his ass off! And this is exactly the situation that we must use to our maximum advantage. We will play with him, just the way he has been playing with us.

"We have now been told that he is in Mumbai. We will tell him, through the media, that we are going to look for him in Mumbai – just as he wants us to. In reality, however, while we *will* send a team to Mumbai just to make sure that we don't slip up, we will beef up our patrolling in the interiors of Karnataka. Especially in Bellary, Tumkur, Chitradurga and the neighbouring areas, from where most of the crimes are being reported. Let us circulate his photos and ask the villagers to be on high alert. Get more manpower, if you need. I am pretty sure that it would not be long before he walks into our trap. Let us talk to the commissioner."

"You are a genius!" Muthuswamy hollered, as he ran towards the commissioner's office. Swaminathan laughed and followed him.

Chapter 26

3rd May 2011

It was the second time in less than a week that Commissioner C. Raghavendra Babu met the press in a crowded room inside the police headquarters. He had to shield his eyes against the flashbulbs and camera lights. There had, however, been a development that warranted a press conference.

He started by reading out a statement for the press.

"The Coimbatore police are closing in on the elusive serial rape accused M. Jaishankar, who is on the run. We have confirmation that the culprit has killed and raped six women in Karnataka over the last forty days. In all, he is presently charged with raping and murdering nineteen women, besides raping seven other women, in the last three years. He is also accused of killing a man and a child in Dharmapuri district in March.

"The Chitradurga district police in Karnataka have pasted pictures of the accused in key public places, including railway stations and bus stands. However, our team has found out that the accused has escaped from Karnataka and *is now in Mumbai.*"

The last sentence gave rise to murmurs in the room.

The commissioner continued, "The special police team from Coimbatore which has now launched a nation-wide man hunt has traced Shankar's mobile phone to Mumbai. The accused has stopped making calls from his mobile as he has realised that the police are after him. We are closing in on him. Our special team has travelled to Mumbai and is working with the Mumbai police to nab him at the earliest," the commissioner ended his statement on a positive note.

Short, stabbing questions started raining down on him.

"One at a time, please," the commissioner said, pointing to a raised arm.

"It has been more than a month and the special team has not been able to arrest the fugitive. How confident are you that the team is looking for the killer in the right places?" asked a reporter.

"I am confident that we are looking in the right places. We have been tracking his location. We are keeping a close watch on areas where incidents similar to his past crimes are being reported from. As we speak, the special team is spread across Salem, Dharmapuri, Bellary, Tumkur, Chitradurga, Bangalore, New Delhi and Mumbai. Over there, yes please," the commissioner pointed at a young woman.

The woman asked, “How is the fugitive managing to travel around, especially to places like Delhi and Mumbai?”

The other journalists started making notes before the commissioner responded.

“We believe that the accused is moving around by trucks. He may be taking up part-time work as a driver or a cleaner. Next, please.”

A young man’s voice. “Is it true that the police have been harassing the family of the accused?”

“That’s not true. We visited the family to check if there was any information that they could help us with. We did it as we found out that the accused had been in touch with his wife. In fact, he stopped calling his wife after we had traced his location to Bangalore.”

“How’s the family dealing with the situation?” – next question.

The commissioner looked into the journalist’s eye and bit his lower lip to restrain his anger. “I cannot make any judgement on that” the commissioner said and stood up, “No more questions, please.”

The room reverberated with more questions, but the commissioner had already walked out.

Chapter 27

4th May 2011

Shankar turned off the engine of the motorbike which he had stolen late in the afternoon. The boy had parked his bike, key in place, on the narrow road that went right through the fields and had walked down a few feet to hide behind the thick bushes by the road and relieve himself. There was no one around, and his need to pee took precedence over his concern for the safety of his bike. He was halfway through his act by the time he had seen Shankar.

While the newspapers did say that the police had traced Shankar's location to Mumbai and had sent a special team to work with Mumbai police, making him some sort of a national celebrity, Shankar sensed heightened police activities in the area. He realised that the police were not taking chances. He reminded himself of the first rule in the life of a fugitive – never stay too long in one place. It was time to move on. He zeroed in on Elagi, a village in the Bijapur district of Karnataka, not too far. He had to change his coordinates quickly.

Shankar could not travel along the main roads. He kept his eyes open on the way, looking out for a car parked where it should not be or someone standing and reading a newspaper under a lamp-post with his eyes on the road, or a man in a shabby dress on a bench looking around. Shankar had not noticed anything of that sort on the way, thankfully. He knew that the police were professionals, and they wielded the wand of authority. That was what scared him the most. The fact that they could carry out their plan, maybe even kill him, and get away without any consequence. The stray bike on the road and the full tank, therefore, came as a boon. By the time the boy had bolted out from behind the bush, hurriedly zipping himself up, the urine splattered on his trousers, the bike could barely be seen through the cloud of dirt and smoke it had left in its trail.

It was late in the evening now. Shankar got off the bike. As soon as the headlight was turned off, it seemed that the darkness smothered him from all sides. He squinted his eyes and looked around. Next to the road, there was a tree with its bare branches, that looked like fingers grasping the moon that hung low over the empty farm by the road. He could see the lights on in a few houses at a distance.

He had stopped at a dhaba a few miles back, and had filled himself with chapati, chicken and cheap liquor. He now felt a different kind of hunger.

As he kept looking around for a prey, he noticed a woman making her way across the farm towards one of the huts.

She was carrying a bag. Must have gone to the local market, Shankar thought. He stepped off the road and followed her with wobbly steps. Should not have drunk like a fish, he reminded himself.

Chandralekha Hotagi stopped in her tracks and turned around. Shankar straightened his shirt, ran his fingers through his dishevelled hair and forced a smile. “Good evening,” he said. “I’ve been on the road since morning, and still have miles to go. I was wondering if I could have some water, and something to eat, if that’s not too much to ask.” The ploy had worked in the past. He hoped that the woman would ask him in and weighed his options. If she were alone, this would prove to be his lucky night. If she had company, he would make a fast exit. If anyone recognised him or otherwise tried to create any problem, then he would have no choice but to get his hands dirty.

He looked closely at Chandralekha. He could not wait to rid her curvaceous body of the cheap saree, which she had wrapped herself in. In his mind, he saw her naked, writhing on the ground, bruised and battered from his merciless beating, as he devoured her body and entered her with brute force. As the salacious images filled his mind, he felt sweat breaking out all over his body, not just from the heat outside and the heavy drinking, but also from the fire burning in his loins.

There was something in the man’s eyes that made Chandralekha uneasy.

"Wait here," she said, "my house is not far. I will get you some food and water."

Shankar realised that the plan had not worked. The bitch was not going to invite him to her house. He had to act right then, and right there!

He grabbed Chandralekha by the arm and pulled her close. Chandralekha cried out in horror. She dropped the bag and clawed Shankar's face, her screams reverberating in the air. Shankar put his hand on her mouth, but it was already too late. Pradeep, Chandralekha's husband, had heard his wife, and came running out of his house. Shankar saw to his horror that the doors and windows of the other houses had also opened, and men and women were running towards him, some of them carrying battery torches. He freed the woman, still crying her lungs out, and turned around. He started running in unsteady steps towards the bike. He had to get away as fast as the alcohol coursing through his blood would allow. The men were catching up.

Shankar looked backwards as he ran. The stone landed on his forehead around the same time that the torches were aimed at his eyes. He turned around and tried to run faster, covering his head with his hands, even as he felt the warmth of the blood trickling down the bridge of his nose, on to his cheek. And then the stones literally rained on him. It seemed that the villagers had made up their mind not to spare even an inch of his body. As he hit the ground, he felt, to his surprise, his eyes filling with tears. The tear ducts were already aware of what Shankar's brain still refused to accept. That he was in deep trouble.

"I am just a police constable, was on duty in plain dress," Shankar said, raising a hand but his feeble voice was lost in the din of the mob which had tasted blood. That face was not unfamiliar to them. They had been seeing that face for the last several days on posters in bus stops, railway stations, and local hotels. There was no mistaking the face that had been haunting them in their nightmares. The monster was squirming on the dust, his arms folded, asking for mercy, as the villagers kept throwing stones at him, beating him up with their sticks, and kicking his balls. Shankar was too shocked, too drunk, too weary to put up a fight against an entire village. His face was smeared with blood. The blood streaming from the wounds above his eyes blurred his vision, and its salty metallic taste filled his mouth. He felt excruciating pain, hoping that the ordeal would soon be over as what seemed like certain and imminent death stared him in the face. The seconds passed. His body began to shake, and his brain started shutting down.

That was when he heard the voices.

"Stop," someone cried out, "stop right now!" He could hear heavy boots running towards the mob.

Then, everything around him became dark and the sounds faded away.

Chapter 28

Some of the villagers sought out and informed the constables patrolling the area. Security in the area had been beefed up over the last few days. After days of sleepless nights with no trace of the fugitive, the constables had almost given up hope. They had begun to believe that the man indeed was Satan himself. He came from nowhere, committed despicable crimes, and then vanished in thin air. So, when they heard that a man who had striking resemblance to the one in the posters, had attacked a woman in the village and had been caught in the act by the villagers, they lost no time and ran to the spot. The man whom the police in Tamil Nadu, Karnataka, Maharashtra and Delhi had been frantically searching for several weeks, was beyond any doubt, a prize catch!

When they reached, they saw that the mob had turned blind with fury. The man on the ground had passed out, but the villagers were still at it. It took the constables some time to disperse the mob and rescue the man. The killer was then taken to the police station at Zalki.

On 5th May 2011, Shankar was handed over to Chitradurga police.

The fugitive had finally run out of luck.

***

Rajaram was part of the special team that arrived at Chitradurga from Coimbatore. He had been asked to identify the fugitive who had escaped from the Salem bus stop, while he, along with Kondasamy, had been escorting him from the Dharmapuri fast-track court to Coimbatore. Rajaram would never forget that face. The last time he had seen the man, he had left him in the company of his roommate Kondasamy at the bus stop, while he had gone to buy tickets for the super deluxe bus in which the bastard had insisted on travelling. Rajaram had had no idea then, that the twenty-five-year-old Kondasamy would kill himself the very next morning, out of shame and fear, after the monster had given them the slip.

When Rajaram now looked at the wounded perpetrator, he could smell the gunpowder that had filled his nostrils on that fateful morning. Kondasamy and he had alighted from the overnight bus at the Bharathiyar Road bus stop near the rear gate of the Police Recruits School and he had been trying his best, often going beyond the boundaries of reason, to pacify his friend, upset over his slip-up at the bus stop the previous night. As he now stared fixedly at the monster, the sound of the gunshot echoed in Rajaram's ears. An icy cold wave ran down his spine, as he remembered the moment when he had turned around hearing the gunshot and had seen his partner lying on the pavement in a pool of blood.

Rajaram looked at the blood-soaked face of the monster in his tattered clothes, and sent out a silent prayer, thanking god that justice had finally been served to his friend Kondasamy.

***

"Jaishankar's recent crimes have largely been committed outside Coimbatore city, and all the cases are under trial before various courts. The only recent case in Tamil Nadu was his escape from Salem. Since Karnataka police require his custody at the moment to probe multiple cases, he will be in judicial and police custody in Karnataka. Tamil Nadu police will seek his custody later," said Commissioner C. Raghavendra Babu to the throng of reporters.

When the reporters had left, the commissioner met with Muthusamy and Swaminathan. He congratulated Muthusamy for successfully leading the special team, and thanked Swaminathan for making the mission successful by sharing his insights into the twisted mind of the killer, and for his innovative plans, that had finally led to the arrest of the fugitive.

However, Swaminathan did not look particularly happy with how the mission had ended.

"I can tell you right now what exactly is going to happen," he told Muthusamy. "Shankar is a cold, calculating monster. He is going to play insane. He is going to create a lot of confusion for the psychologists. It might happen that he will not be sent to prison. He might end up in a psychiatric ward, and he will show such tremendous progress in the next few years, that he will be released. That is how it is now, Muthu. That is how we deal with the scum of the society. We do not clean it up, we do not throw it away. We just move it around a bit here and a bit there. And when we discover that the house is stinking, it is already too late and the house is infested by the rats. We have become so soft and nice that no one dares to take the responsibility for doing what might be perceived as being 'unpleasant'."

Muthusamy looked at the horizon, feeling sad. The killer was now in the custody of Karnataka police, and only time would tell what destiny had in store for the man.

As Swaminathan got ready to leave, Muthusamy hugged him and said, "Swamy, I know we wouldn't have made it without you. Now, go back to your family and take a break. We all need one badly!"

Swaminathan smiled absent-mindedly.

***

Shankar was lodged in Central Prisons, Parappana Agrahara jail in Bangalore, Karnataka, on 5th May, 2011. There were now against him, thirteen rape and murder cases and an additional seven rape cases in Tamil Nadu for which he was being tried before his escape from Salem. To add to those, six rape and murder cases in Bellary in Karnataka and two murder cases in Dharmapuri in Tamil Nadu, along with several other allegations of rape and murder in the Tumkur and Chitradurga districts in Karnataka after his escape. It was also decided that he would be undergoing treatment for psychiatric problems.

However, what the Karnataka police did not know was that their worst nightmare had just started.

PART FIVE

THE GREAT ESCAPE

Chapter 29

When the Karnataka state government decided to convert the twenty-two-acre premises of the old Bangalore Jail into the Freedom Park, the news made headlines. Since the time it had been built during the British rule in 1867, the jail had, over the years, housed freedom fighters, as well as some of the most notorious criminals the state had ever seen. A budget of ten crores was approved for the necessary renovation. The city corporation had realised that the grounds would be an ideal location for a park, thanks to its proximity to the Bangalore Race Course. It was also decided that a five-acre area within the park would be earmarked for holding rallies and protests, just as the Hyde Park in London offers a similar arrangement for those who need to raise their voices against the system from time to time. There was never a dearth of matters to protest against. The architects, chosen through a nationwide contest, wanted to retain the old barracks and hospital blocks as heritage centres, standing next to children's play areas, jogging tracks, museums, souvenir shops and light-and-sound shows. The old prison records would also be retained for their historical value.

The old jail was shut down in 2000, and a new one, established in 1997, became the Bangalore Central Prison, also known as Parappana Agrahara jail. That was now the address of dreaded serial rapist and killer M. Jaishankar. He had been convicted in two cases of rape and murder in Hiriyur, a small town near Chitradurga in Karnataka.

Shankar took time to get used to life inside the Bangalore Central Prison, a world by itself that had its own rules and conventions. The prison stretched over forty acres of land, much like the farmlands nearby. The jail was a gigantic structure with high perimeter walls, barbed wire fencing and dull grey granite blocks. However, it was bursting at the seams with prisoners, almost double its planned capacity. The dark cells inside were overcrowded, and yet, lonely.

To manage the population within the jail, the authorities frequently freed undertrials and convicts on a variety of grounds that ranged from good behaviour to lack of sufficient evidence for conviction. However, the flow of prisoners never stopped. The jail was always running short of staff, who had the arduous task of keeping an eye on the hordes of prisoners. The police played gods, the system and the society having given them the authority to rule over the lives of inmates holed up in dingy, dark cells.

Shankar saw convicts walking around listlessly, the men in their coarse cotton shirts and pyjamas, the women in their sarees, their lives and very existence owned by the khaki-clad jail warders who called the shots. The prisoners shared the meagre food, the dirty bathrooms and kitchen, and stood in never-ending queues before the handful of tube wells within the premises. Some of the inmates attended rudimentary classes of moral science, aimed at cleansing their souls. They worked for paltry wages of ten or twenty rupees a day, making wooden furniture, or weaving khadi dresses. The wages were in the form of coupons which they could redeem to buy food or other necessities which the jail did not provide by default. Sometimes, they could also be used to buy favours from some of the warders, who did not mind some earnings on the side.

Shankar looked at the men playing *hulikattu* outside the cells, using pebbles like pawns in a game of chess, on a board carved out on the grey floors. He never joined them, and they never invited him. Shankar did not complain but often wondered why. Were they afraid of him? Did they hate him for what he had done? Well, none of them was an epitome of virtue himself!

Unlike Shankar, most of the inmates had given in to despair and had nothing to look forward to. Because they knew that the jail would not redeem or repair them, but would simply scar them for life, marking them as 'different' from the law-abiding citizens outside. When they were freed from the jail, most of them would be shunned by family and friends. Most of them would go back to doing whatever had thrown them behind bars in the first place. Shankar, however, had no time to wallow in self-pity. He had plans. He explored and observed every nook and cranny of the jail compound, making mental notes that would one day set in motion his grand plan. A plan that had to be executed at the earliest because the warm winds of the highways still beckoned him.

He had managed to gain the trust of most of the staffers in the jail – to the extent where some of them even entrusted him with the duty of opening and locking the doors in the barracks every morning and evening. Among the handful of inmates Shankar got along with in jail was Abdul Rahim Pasha, who stayed in a barrack next to Shankar's. A site supervisor by profession, he had been remanded in judicial custody on a dowry harassment charge in 2012, but maintained that he had been framed. What Shankar liked about Pasha was the fact that he never judged. Not too many questions, never fishing for details. Shankar always liked a man who gave the monster inside him its space.

There were days when Pasha told him stories. In fact, the jail was abuzz with interesting stories. Shankar came to know about a nun who visited the cells every day and spoke to the prisoners, trying to lift them from the quagmire of despair and enlighten their miserable lives with hope and faith. There had been a convict named Victor, who left the jail a reformed man and started working as a plumber after he was released. There was a thirty-year-old woman, an engineer from Mumbai, who was serving a sentence along with her husband who held a management degree, both arrested on charges of theft. The couple had been ostracised by their parents and relatives and had a five-year-old son growing up in the dark and dangerous world within the four walls of the prison. There was another woman, who had been charged with a murder she claimed she had never committed, but had been framed by her husband, who had wanted to get rid of her, so that he could be with another woman. And then, there was the happy-go-lucky sixty-year-old 'white man' who had been arrested for carrying seven kilograms of hashish, who did not mind his court hearings getting regularly postponed. He had made friends here and had generally come to like his life in the Indian prison.

In Pasha, Shankar had found a friend in the most unlikely of places. But that was what life was like! It could be a bitch one moment, and a sweetheart in the next. Shankar had asked for Pasha's mobile phone number. He would get in touch with his friend when he was out. He was the man who, Shankar felt, could be relied upon.

Shankar knew that the walls of the Bangalore Central Jail would not be able to hold him back for long.

Chapter 30

On 25th July 2008, the city of Bangalore was rocked by nine bomb blasts that killed two persons and injured at least twenty. The blast was caused by low-intensity crude bombs triggered by timers. A joint team of Karnataka police and Kerala police arrested Abdul Nasser Madani, an Islamic cleric and the leader of People's Democratic Party (PDP), Kerala, from his residence in the Kollam district of Kerala on 17th August 2010 in connection with the 2008 serial blasts in Bangalore. When he was lodged in the Bangalore Central Prison, Madani did not know that his stay in the jail would coincide with the most sensational jailbreak in the history of the region. He was lodged on the ground floor of the hospital block, where Shankar, along with other convicts and undertrials, who were considered mentally challenged or had other illnesses, had also been put up.

On Saturday, 31st August 2013, Shankar had been taken to a court in Tumkur for a hearing in a rape and murder case. He was escorted back to his prison cell in the hospital block on his return. Shankar stayed on the second floor of the hospital block. The cells were under constant vigil by three convict watchmen. Due to the paucity of guards in the jail, the prison department often entrusted those serving life imprisonments in the jail with the task of guarding other prisoners. As a procedure, the watchmen locked Shankar in his cell every evening by six and handed the key over to a security guard who was posted outside the hospital block. To maximise security, the locks in the cells could be opened only from the outside.

On his return from the court in Tumkur, Shankar said that he felt uneasy. A doctor from the prison hospital visited him in his cell in the evening.

1st September 2013

It was around two in the night.

The cell reverberated with the relentless snoring of Bore Gowda. Tonight, for a change, Shankar did not complain about his cell-mate's nocturnal orchestra that deprived him of peaceful sleep every night. He was wide awake, keeping an eye on the movement of the guards outside his cell. They came by to inspect his cell every half an hour. A round had just been completed, which meant that there would be no one in the vicinity of the cell in the next thirty minutes. He had the next thirty minutes to himself. Those were the thirty minutes during which he would have to put into action the plans he had been firming up in his mind over the past six months. The last two months had been especially difficult. He had had to drill down to the nitty-gritty, conduct a recce of the premises on several occasions, consider every possible manner in which things could go wrong and plan workarounds, and most importantly, buy the favours of a few individuals within the jail.

Shankar hastily put on the police uniform which was carefully hidden under his pillow. Next, he picked up the white bedsheet. Finally, he fished out the makeshift key. Thankfully, the lock was within his reach. The 'key' could only open the lock, but Shankar did not mind.

Shankar tip-toed his way out of his cell, taking care not to wake up Bore Gowda, and ran down the stairs to the ground floor. The corridors were empty. The prisoners inside the ground floor cells, including the PDP leader, were fast asleep. The only sound Shankar could hear was that of his own heart pounding against his ribs. Thankfully, he had not run into any of the guards so far. He crossed the corridor in brisk steps till he reached the door at the far end. The door was open, just as he had expected. Beyond that door, there was a small waiting area, which opened to the lawn outside. The door leading to the lawn had been left open as well.

Shankar smiled. He was glad that they had kept their word. He had realised long back that it would not be possible to make his way out of the jail on his own, and that he would have to win a few people over to his side to help him. That was the only problem with his plan – the fact that it hinged on the honesty of others. Honesty and fairness, he had always known for certain, could be bought over with money but did not come with guarantees. That had been bothering him all these months. But this had indeed looked like his lucky night so far.

Now he heaved a sigh of relief as he walked out of the hospital block into the cool damp air of the night, unchallenged and unscathed. A black cat scurrying across the lawn stopped in its tracks, scrutinised the prisoner with a long, cold stare and then went about its business. That, however, was one witness Shankar would not lose his sleep over.

Shankar knew this part of the prison like the back of his hand. He could find his way around even with his eyes closed. He would have to run fifty metres before he reached the banana garden. He knew that next to the garden, there was a pile of wooden planks and other materials that were being used for the construction work that had been going on in that part of the prison for quite some time.

Shankar ran across the banana garden towards the twenty feet high wall. The grass under his feet was wet and the trees swayed their heads in the breeze. A dog barked somewhere, disrupting the monotonous cacophony of insects. He was now a few minutes away from the moment he had been waiting for, for more than a year. He would soon be a free man once again! He threw away the crude duplicate key of his cell when he reached the bottom of the wall. He looked around. The wooden slats, the piles of bricks, and the bamboo sticks from the scaffolding had not been removed. Almost breathless with excitement, Shankar climbed atop the wall. He had not felt an adrenaline rush like he did now for months, and it was making him do the unthinkable.

Shankar looked behind his shoulder one more time. The hospital block with its occupants fast asleep stood silently behind him, forming a dark silhouette on the night sky. The inner wall gave way to a perpendicular wall around fifteen feet high, which connected it with the compound wall, which was more than thirty feet high. Shankar walked quickly down the narrow top of the connecting wall, crouching, breathing hard through his mouth, trying to hide from any policeman who had not sold his soul and who might see him. He was sweating profusely, and there were patches of sweat on the police uniform he was wearing.

Shankar used the bedsheet to make a padding over the glass pieces on the top, as he walked a few feet along the wall. He knew that the perimeter wall had electric fencing – the last hurdle which could change his destiny forever, either way. He wondered if the money he had spent on those policemen had been enough to keep their moral scruples off the way and the electric current off the barbwire.

Shankar removed his belt. He tied the bedsheet to the belt and flung it over the harmless barbwire to the outer side of the perimeter wall. He then tied the leather belt firmly to an iron post on the fence. He crawled out through the barbwire, even as it cut through the uniform and then through his flesh, drawing blood. He bit his lips to keep himself from crying out loud and grabbed the bedsheet. He looked down and could see nothing but darkness. Shankar started climbing down, the wind whistling past his ears. He knew that there was muddy ground outside the wall on this side of the jail, and when he was about ten feet from the ground, he would jump.

His heart skipped a beat when he felt the bedsheet giving way under his weight.

Chapter 31

Shankar landed on his back with a dull thud. He had not made it to the muddy terrain that was just a few feet away from where gravity had pulled him down instead, his fingers still firmly clutching an end of the bedsheet which had torn across the middle.

As he fell on the rough, gravelly ground adjacent to the wall, Shankar thought he heard the ominous, crunching sound of his bones breaking. It seemed as if a pall of cold darkness had wrapped him on all sides. For a few minutes, he could not breathe, and his limbs felt numb. And then, the sharp pain exploded inside his body, and spread all over like wildfire. Shards of broken glass had penetrated the soles of his feet. The relentless bleeding now formed blackish red rivulets that stained the stones on which he had landed. The fugitive lay outside the prison wall, constantly shivering and occasionally retching, the spasms in his muscles sweeping across his body.

As Shankar closed his eyes, he saw himself behind the wheel, before him empty roads cutting through dark forests, and at his feet his black bag with the machete stained by the blood of a woman he had just savoured to his heart's content and hacked to death. But even as he was sinking irreversibly into unconsciousness, a voice inside kept reminding him that he was the master of his destiny outside the walls of prison, and he had very little time to get back on his own two feet and run as far away from the prison as he could, before the skies cleared and a new day began.

***

When Bode Gowda woke up the next morning, it was already past seven. He had slept well, without any disturbance. The maniac with whom he had to share his cell by cruel designs of fate, had not snored at all last night. Where was he, by the way? Gowda looked around the cell and his eyes went to the door. It was unlocked!

He sat up straight and called out Shankar's name a few times. There was no response. Then, he stood up and went to the open door of the cell. There was no trace of Shankar outside.

A few days back, something similar had happened. Shankar was neither inside the cell, nor anywhere outside in its vicinity. The staffers panicked and started looking for him everywhere in the prison compound. He was finally found in the gardens between the hospital block and the inner security wall. "What do you think you are doing here?" asked an angry guard. "I was feeling hungry and came here to pluck some fruits," pat came Shankar's nonchalant reply.

"The bastard has probably gone out to the garden to get fruits again," thought Gowda. He could see a guard at the far end of the corridor, gossiping with another. “Shankar is not inside,” he said loudly as he walked towards the guards. One of them joked, “Must have gone for his fruit salad.”

Chapter 32

In no time, the premises of the Bangalore Central Jail was teeming with khaki-clad policemen and jail warders. The morning sun was beating down on the city, and everything around was bright and shiny. However, the most wanted criminal of the region seemed to have evaporated, as if by a magician's trick. Something like that had happened for the first time in the history of the Central Prison since its inception in 1997. The Bangalore police took pride, and justifiably so, in the stringent security of the Central Prison. That pride had been made to lick the dust a few hours ago.

The police had initially assumed that there was no way Shankar had been able to get out of the jail premises. He must have been hiding somewhere inside the prison complex, waiting for the right opportunity to escape. Therefore, the search party had zealously spread out in different directions, sweating it out in the sun, combing through every inch of the barracks and the lawns, but there was no trace of Shankar. Finally, the police, baffled and clueless, accepted the fact that the impossible might have happened after all. Shankar had managed to escape from the jail.

The teams started scanning the areas around the perimeter walls for any possible clue. At two places within the jail premises, there were walls connecting the inner wall with the outer compound wall. Those would be the ideal places for someone to use as escape routes. If you could somehow scale the inner wall, there was already a path, however hazardous, that led straight to the thirty-feet high outer wall. The search for clues was now focused on those two places. The police started with the garden around fifty metres away from the hospital block where Shankar had been lodged, as that would be the most likely route that Shankar might have taken. They also took into account the fact that Shankar had been found loitering in that area a few days back. They struck gold in no time.

It started with the discovery of the key. A prison guard named Ramesh had been rummaging through the undergrowth inside the garden, when his eyes caught the light reflected from a metallic object in the grass. Squinting his eyes, Ramesh walked to the source of light and picked up what looked like a crude key. He picked it up and ran to the head warder who was leading the group. "Looks like a key. We need to test this on the lock of Shankar's cell right away. This could be the key with which he had opened the lock, and then thrown it away while scaling the wall," the head warder said. As Ramesh ran towards the hospital block, the team was now convinced that Shankar must have sneaked out by scaling the wall next to the banana garden.

In no time, a ladder was fetched, and one of the guards started climbing up. When he reached the top of the inner wall, his eyes went to the perpendicular wall that connected it to the outer wall. There were glass pieces on top of the wall, and in the bright sunlight, there was no mistaking the reddish black stains on them. Shankar must have bled as he had walked along that wall. Next, his eyes went to the top of the perimeter wall. There was a belt tied to one of the iron posts, with a bedsheet tied to it, and flung over the wall. Shankar must have used that sheet to climb down. "How did the bastard cross the electric barbwire?" the guard wondered aloud.

The team rushed out to inspect the area outside the wall, where Shankar must have landed.

Chapter 33

Joint Commissioner of Police (Law and Order) Vijay Krishna Singh had received a call from the Commissioner of Police Manavendra Agarkar twenty minutes back. He had been asked to join an emergency meeting, and it had not taken VK, as he was popularly called long, to understand that this had to be something very serious. As he walked into the room and looked around the table, his doubt was confirmed.

He could see Commissioner Manavendra Agarkar, Additional Commissioner of Police (Law and Order) Amal Pant, Additional Deputy General of Police (Prisons), K.V. Amandeep, and at the head of the table, the Home Minister K.J. George himself. The Commissioner looked first at VK, and then at the home minister and said, "Sir, Joint Commissioner V.K. Singh will lead the team." VK had barely had the time to pull a chair and take his seat.

He looked questioningly around the table, trying desperately to figure out what exactly he had just been put in charge of. The ADGP (Prisons), K.V. Amandeep, understood his predicament and said, "VK, we have had an incident last night. M. Jaishankar has escaped from the Central Prison.

We are putting together a team with the bests among us. You will be in charge of the operation."

The home minister turned towards VK and said, "The commissioner has spoken very highly of you and I am sure you will manage to get the killer back behind bars very soon," at which VK turned towards the commissioner and lowered his head in a gesture of gratitude as the home minister continued with his eyes sweeping around the table. "Can anyone of you tell me how people choose their leaders?"

No one spoke. VK saw the commissioner fiddle with the knot of his tie.

"It is not charisma, it is not charm as a lot of us would like to believe," the home minister continued, "it is trust. The key word is 'trust'. People select the leaders they trust, and when we are sent to the highest offices in the state or the country, there is an implicit expectation that we would keep the people safe. That is the faith they have in the leaders they elect, and we rely on you, the police, to make sure that the trust with which people elect us is never broken. You are the custodians of law and order, and when something like this happens, the faith of the people is endangered. That, I am sure all of you will agree, is not a good thing."

The policemen around the table lowered their heads.

"The fact of the matter is that as we speak, a man, accused in more than thirty gruesome rape and murder cases, is on the loose in the heart of Bangalore city. This has happened because of lapses on your part. This does not make you look good. This does not make me look good. And we need to fix this as soon as we can. Even the man on the street understands that we have been caught napping while the most dangerous prisoner of the Central Jail scaled the walls in the middle of the night and ran away.

"So, my advice to you is that do not even try to find excuses. Accept your mistake before the public. Find out those among you who helped the man escape. I am not ready to believe that the prisoner escaped from a high security prison without help from within. Make sure that you get to the root of this and serve exemplary punishment to those who are found to be at fault. And go all out to find the killer. All this, while assuring the people of safety and a good night's sleep. Makes sense?"

"You have my word, sir," said the commissioner. There was affirmation around the table. "We have already created the blueprint of a plan," the commissioner continued. "We are going to spread out into twelve separate teams to hunt down the killer. Joint Commissioner V.K. Singh will have central control. ADGP K.V. Amandeep has already initiated an investigation into the likely involvement of jail staff. I will keep you updated on the progress."

"Sounds like a plan," the home minister smiled and stood up. "Let us get to work," he said as he left the room with the commissioner and the additional commissioner seeing him out.

Chapter 34

The reporter from *The News of India* raised her voice above the cacophony in the room and asked, "Sir, how exactly did this happen?"

The commissioner cleared his throat and got ready to speak as the flashguns of cameras and the bright lights almost blinded him. For a fraction of a second, the words of the honourable home minister rang in his ears. There was no point trying to absolve the police of the charges of negligence. He was going to say it, just the way it had happened. He said, "Jaishankar had got hold of a duplicate key to the hospital cell where he had been locked up. He had noticed that the guards came to inspect his cell every half an hour and he knew that he had a thirty-minute window to escape from his cell. Once a round of inspection by the guards had been over at around two in the night, Jaishankar opened his cell door with the duplicate key.

"After leaving his cell, Jaishankar went to the ground floor and then to the garden. There, he scaled a twenty-foot wall, then walked atop a fifteen-foot connecting wall and then scaled the thirty-foot high perimeter wall. On reaching the perimeter wall, he used a belt and a bedsheet which he had stolen from the hospital."

The commissioner sighed as he finished his statement. The cameramen went crazy. Every reporter in the room tried to shout above everyone else.

"What do you have to say about the obvious lapses inside the Central Prison? A retired superintendent of the Central Prison has gone on record saying that senior officers in the jail are directly responsible for the jailbreak. He had observed Shankar's frequent movements outside the prison cell. He has told us that he did warn the jail authorities, but no one paid heed to his warning," a reporter from *Daily Times* shot the question at ADGP K.V. Amandeep. The retired superintendent of the Central Prison had also drawn the attention of the reporters to serious systemic problems inside the jail, which needed to be attended to on an urgent basis. He had mentioned that there were at least thirty old locks being used in the prison, which could be easily opened with a single key. Also, some smart prisoners could open locks using wires, if such locks were within their reach, like the locks in the cells in the hospital block were.

Amandeep stirred in his seat and with the same spirit as the commissioner said, "I would not deny the possibility of involvement of insiders and our lapses in certain areas. In fact, preliminary investigation has indeed revealed negligence on the part of a few subordinate officers that led to Jaishankar's escape sometime between 1 a.m. and 4 a.m.

"Apparently, Jaishankar escaped wearing a police uniform. We need to find out how he got hold of one! The key that Jaishankar used to open the lock of his prison cell could have been made by him or with the help of someone else in the jail. The prison guards had been careless and had left open two gates leading from the hospital to the garden. This is absolutely unacceptable. He then used a connecting wall to reach the compound wall – in fact, there are two such walls in the premises. As a corrective measure, I have ordered both of those walls to be taken down this morning. The electric fencing was also not functional that night. I have already made enquiries and have confirmed that there was no power cut that night. An officer of ASP rank was in charge of the infrastructure. He had not checked the system or reported any malfunction to the jail authorities. He is in suspension now."

"So, what have you done about these lapses?" the reporter screamed.

"Based on findings from preliminary enquiries, we have currently suspended eleven individuals – two jailors, three wardens and six security guards." Amandeep read out the names of the eleven who had been suspended and were being interrogated. He then added, "Let us, however, be aware of some of the systemic and logistical challenges we have. The Bangalore Central prison has forty CCTV cameras, of which only eight are in working condition. Though there are more than fifty high-risk inmates at the moment who need monitoring round the clock, the prison staff has been managing with only eight cameras in the cells."

There was a murmur around the room. Another reporter said, "We have just been informed that a committee, headed by the home secretary, is being set up to probe the security lapses in the Central Prison, including the possibility of insider involvement. What do you have to say about that?"

"We will cooperate with the committee," the commissioner replied.

The reporters then turned to VK, who had earlier been introduced by the commissioner as the man in charge of the operation. VK looked at the commissioner and the ADGP, Prisons. He liked the manner in which the two had honoured the request from the home minister. They had admitted the lapses inside the prison, and had come clean before the people, also assuring them that action had already been initiated against the suspected policemen. However, VK did not have any intention of divulging the details of the plan that he had been working on with his teams over the last few hours. The last thing he wanted was to have the details of his action plan plastered all over the town or blaring out from television screens. He believed in following a strict no-disclosure policy when it came to handling sensitive missions. The media did not have to be his messenger to the fugitive.

"I can assure the people of Bangalore that my team and I would do everything we can to keep them safe. Jaishankar would be back in Central Prison very soon," VK kept it short and stood up, along with the other officials, to leave. The reporters did not mind his brevity. They had already got enough fodder for one day.

Chapter 35

It was getting dark and Arthi started walking faster. Her mathematics tutorial had run longer than usual. She had not been able to get one of those geometry problems right and the teacher, an enthusiastic young Tamilian man, would not let her go unless she had completed her assignment.

The sky was clear, and the trees surrounding the small fishermen's hamlet near Kudlu Gate swayed in the cool evening breeze. Arthi could hear a variety of familiar sounds from the houses that lined the narrow road – the daily soaps and news bulletins on television, children reading from their textbooks, the blaring of radio sets, girls practising music on their harmoniums, women cooking meals for the night in kitchens.

As the houses along the road became fewer and far between, the sounds died down slowly, as if an invisible hand had turned the volume down on the symphony of life, which had so far been comforting and reassuring Arthi, the late hour notwithstanding. As she now looked ahead, she could see the empty field and the lights in the windows of her house on the other side. The road went by the temple that stood right in the middle of the field.

As Arthi approached the temple, she could feel her heart beating faster. All she could hear were the insects and the occasional night birds. Her eyes kept looking for the man who had taken shelter in the temple since the last two days. There was something about the way the man stared at her every time she passed by the temple that sent a shiver down her spine.

The man had close-cropped hair, his clothes were tattered, and he had bruises all over. There was a piece of cloth tied clumsily around each of his feet. There were blood stains on them. The man barely moved around and could be found lying on the temple steps most of the time. She had heard that some of the villagers had seen him lying on the school grounds a few days back. He had moved to the temple, as they had shooed him away from the school grounds. He appeared to be in severe pain.

As Arthi crossed the temple clutching her books tightly on her chest, she saw him on the steps, just as she had expected. The man was lying on his stomach, his face turned towards the road. As soon as he saw Arthi, he tried to get up, but he could not. He grimaced and fell back on his stomach, his eyes not leaving the sixteen-year-old even for a second.

Arthi started running and did not stop till she reached her house and rang the doorbell. As she shut her eyes tight, gasping for breath, the menacing eyes of the tramp on the temple steps, glowing in the dark, flashed in her mind.

Who the hell was that man, and what was he doing in the village?

Chapter 36

"How long are you going to stay here?" asked the boy from the local restaurant who brought Shankar food every night, as he counted the change. Shankar had moved away from the temple and had put up in a deserted shack by the Nagendra Reddy Lake the previous night. The temple had too many visitors throughout the day, and Shankar could not risk being seen in the premises. He was sure that the police had launched a manhunt for him, and his face was up there on posters across the city. However, having cropped his hair and removed his beard and moustache, he looked like a different man. One could not blame the villagers for the fact that the fugitive had not already been handed over to the police and thrown behind bars.

The shack was still a much better alternative. It had originally been built as a resting place for the fishermen who came to the lake. It was hidden away from prying eyes inside a grove by the lake. The tall trees surrounding the shack gave it shade, and also helped Shankar avoid the trouble of having to answer probing questions from curious villagers. He did not have to worry about his daily supply of water as well. He himself had no idea how long it would take to arrange for a vehicle to run away from that god-forsaken village. Till such time, he had no choice but to stay in hiding.

"Till the time my wounds are healed," Shankar replied to the boy's question curtly, making it amply clear that he was not interested in continuing the conversation. The boy nodded, kept staring at him for some time and then ran away. The dark shack by the lake with its musty odour, and that tramp with the eyes of a mad man – both gave him the creeps.

The boy had not been the first one in the village to ask Shankar who he was, what had brought him there, and how long he would stay in the village. It was, after all, a small hamlet where people knew each other, and the arrival of a wounded stranger had not gone unnoticed.

In the story that Shankar had woven, he was a poor truck driver from Tamil Nadu, who moved goods across the states. "I have been driving for three nights in a row. On the third night, the truck had an accident on the highway near Bommanahalli. I was badly hurt. I managed to reach your village and I cannot travel any further at this time," he recited the same account to whoever cared to listen. However, every time someone asked him how he had turned up at the village, he remembered the night he had escaped from the Central Prison.

Shankar had fainted from the impact of the fall and did not know how long he had lain outside the compound wall of the prison. When he came back to his senses, he looked around himself as he lay still on the stones. No frenzied sauntering of guards, no frenetic blowing of whistles. The night was as quiet as it had been when the bedsheet had snapped and brought him down to the ground. They had not found out yet.

It was still not too late. He still stood a chance.

However, it would not be long before Shankar was missed. He had to move away as far as he could in the shortest possible time. When he tried to get up on his feet, the pain made him wince. He kept himself from crying out by biting his lips. He looked at his feet. The soles were bleeding, and his feet were swollen. On top of that the pain in his back was killing him. He could barely stand straight for more than a few minutes. There was no way he could walk too far away from the jail.

Limping and crawling alternately, Shankar barely made it to the village near Kudlu Gate before the day dawned. He could proceed no further. The exhaustion was almost killing him. He got rid of the khaki shirt and decided to stay in hiding in the village for a few days before his wounds healed and he got back the strength to go further away.

As Shankar now lay wide awake inside the shack after washing down his frugal meal with the water from the lake, he was worried. He had managed to carry only five hundred rupees with him when he had escaped from jail, and the money he was left with was fast running out. At this rate, he would not be able to survive for long. Also, thanks to the backache and the wounds on his feet, he was not able to do odd jobs like he had done when he had escaped from prison on the previous occasion.

In the Central Prison, every prisoner was given a BSNL SIM card. They could call their family and friends on their mobile phones at fixed times during the day, and for fixed durations. After Pasha had been released, Shankar used to call him frequently using the SIM card provided by the jail authorities. In fact, Pasha visited him a few times in the jail. He had also given Shankar some money, which the latter had judiciously used to win over some of the guards. Shankar had made up his mind that if there was one person he would get in touch with after running away from the prison, that would be Pasha.

In his current situation, Shankar needed money. More importantly, he needed a motorbike, although he was still not confident of being able to ride one. He was certain that Pasha would be able to help him. The man had appeared to be resourceful.

Shankar badly needed to get in touch with his friend. The question was how. He was not carrying a phone as he did not want the police to track his movements.

Chapter 37

"*Beware! Psycho Killer on the Loose!*" screamed the headline of one of the most prominent dailies in Karnataka.

The state was in the grip of terror. There was every reason to be, as the police apprehended that history might repeat itself. The last time Shankar had escaped, he had been charged with the rape-and-murder of six women in the Bellary district, two murders in Dharmapuri in Tamil Nadu, and several incidents of rape-and-murder had been reported from Tumkur and Chitradurga districts of Karnataka – all in the span of forty-five days before he was captured while trying to rape another woman in the Bijapur district.

VK believed that Shankar would definitely visit quacks or doctors to get treated before he managed to escape very far away from the Central Prison. He therefore decided to alert neighbouring police stations and hospitals. The police issued a lookout notice, which was sent to hospitals in the city and its outskirts. The notice mentioned that M. Jaishankar had escaped from the Bangalore Central Prison by scaling first, the inner wall and then the northern perimeter wall. While escaping, it was likely that Shankar had sustained bleeding injuries due to the penetration of pieces of glass into the soles of his feet, as well as abrasive injuries on other parts of his body. The injured fugitive might visit doctors at clinics, hospitals, or nursing homes under assumed names. If a doctor had reason to suspect any of the patients, the police should be informed as soon as possible.

VK was in a dilemma. On the one hand, he was worried about the security of women in the state capital and the neighbouring areas in the wake of Shankar's escape. On the other hand, he did not want to create panic among the people of the state. He had to make a choice. He decided in favour of the former. Based on his track record, it was highly probable that the sex maniac would start targeting solitary women. A red alert was issued. Working women or those who travelled by themselves were urged to be careful, especially in isolated places. Police stations across the state were alerted and were asked to beef up patrolling in such places where the monster was likely to strike.

The police announced a reward of five lakhs to anybody who could provide information leading to Shankar's arrest. They printed ten thousand posters and seventy-five thousand pamphlets with different photographic profiles of Shankar in five different languages - Hindi, Kannada, Marathi, Tamil and Telugu. The news of his escape along with his photographs were printed in every newspaper and were aired on radios and television channels. The police teams started checking all kinds of vehicles at the state borders.

"Let's also spread the net over Tamil Nadu, Andhra Pradesh and Kerala. The last time when he escaped from the Salem bus depot in Tamil Nadu, he fled to our state. The bastard moves around in trucks, mainly along the national and state highways. Pay special attention to the highways. Make sure that the pamphlets are distributed in all truck terminals and fuel stations," the commissioner advised VK when two days had passed and there was no trace of Shankar.

Women barely moved out of the safe confines of their homes. Those who had to step out for work returned early. The roads looked deserted after eight in the night. Rumours began to fly thick and fast. It was said that the serial killer knew black magic. How else did he fool all the guards and escape from a high-security prison? It was also suggested that the monster hypnotised his victims before raping and killing them. The satanic magician could be lurking anywhere in the dark and could appear before a hapless victim anytime. The entire police force across the state had not been able to catch him yet, because he could melt into the night. Therefore, the wisest thing to do was to stay indoors. The Hotagi family in Bijapur, who was instrumental in getting him arrested the last time, was scared that Shankar might go back to them for revenge. They lived in fear, although the police had arranged for patrolling in the area.

As more and more people became scared and suspicious, the false alarms started ringing.

On Tuesday, 3rd September, the Ramanagar police received information that a person resembling Jaishankar had been seen near the Byramangala Gate on Mysore Road. A team headed by Deputy Superintendent of Police (Ramanagar), Ramalingappa, immediately rushed to the spot, and scoured the area, but did not find the man. The police conducted inquiries and found out that the alarm had been raised after a homeless person with tattered clothes had been seen in the area. "We do not want to take any chances. We have formed search teams, and we are searching for Jaishankar around Ramanagar," Ramalingappa later told the press.

On Wednesday, 4th September, the police received numerous calls from people reporting the movement of suspicious persons. A panicked woman from Anekal alerted the police about the movement of a person near her house. The police immediately picked him up and questioned him. It turned out to be yet another false alarm.

On the same day, in Vellore, the police detained a mentally challenged person for over twenty-four hours as he resembled Jaishankar. Though the embarrassed police later admitted it to be a case of mistaken identity, the youth, who was later identified as a certain Dharmendra from Lucknow, was kept in police custody till late in the night. There was also report of a detention at a hospital in Hosur, Tamil Nadu, which turned out to be erroneous.

Every time there was a report, the excitement in the team was palpable. The police jumped into action with renewed vigour and enthusiasm, only to be disappointed.

VK decided to consult the officers who had nabbed the elusive killer in the past. VK lost no time in calling up Inspector Muthuswamy of Coimbatore Police, and Inspector Swaminathan from Tirupur where the saga had started. VK had done his homework on the case and knew that Swaminathan, in particular, had a thorough understanding of the manner in which the killer's mind worked. Swaminathan had, in the past, foreseen the actions of the killer, and had helped the police stay a step ahead of him, eventually leading to his arrest the last time around.

"We are combing through the state borders. We are also working very closely with the police from neighbouring states, especially in Tamil Nadu," VK told Swaminathan. "Do you think he might have escaped to his old hunting grounds in Tamil Nadu, knowing that the Karnataka police has launched a manhunt for him in the state?"

Swaminathan had arrived in Bangalore to help the Karnataka police in their hunt for Shankar. He thought for a while and said, "That does seem like a natural course of action for a fugitive. But let us not forget the fact that this is a man who is badly wounded. I believe it is unlikely that he has managed to escape to places like Krishnagiri, Hosur or Dharmapuri in Tamil Nadu, if those are the places you are referring to as his old hunting ground. I have a feeling that he is still in Karnataka, possibly somewhere not very far from the prison, injured and weak, waiting for the right time and means to escape."

"Unlike last time, he is not using a mobile phone, making it impossible for us to track his movements," VK said.

Swaminathan smiled and said, "The last time, he used his mobile phone as a ploy to confuse the police. We tracked his location down to the interiors of Karnataka and then to Bangalore. Then, suddenly he appeared to be roaming around in places like New Delhi and Mumbai, even as he wreaked havoc right here in Karnataka. He would not repeat that tactic. He knows that he cannot fool the police twice with the same trick.

"Besides, who would he even call for help, even if he had a phone? He knows that his family doesn't care for him. His wife would only be too happy to hand him over to the police. With the eyes of the entire nation on this case, none of his friends, if he has any left, would come forward to pull him out of his misery. But Shankar now needs a friend more than ever to bail him out. Who would he call if he had a phone?"

Swaminathan ran his fingers through his hair as he sipped his coffee. Suddenly, as an idea struck him, he looked up at VK and said, "He must have used the SIM card provided by the jail while he was here. Let us find out whom he called from jail, especially in the days before his escape! That may give us some clues."

The two policemen sprang to their feet.

PART SIX

CURTAINS

Chapter 38

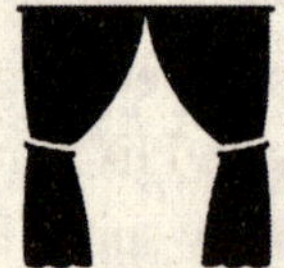

"We have looked into the numbers which Shankar called from the jail regularly, and you are the one he called most frequently," VK looked into the eyes of Abdul Rahim Pasha, who sat in front of him across the table.

The police had examined the call records of the BSNL SIM card which Shankar had been using inside the jail. They had found that the person whom Shankar had been constantly in touch with, even three days before his escape from the jail, was Pasha, whom he had befriended in jail.

There was no other sound in the room, except the creaking of the ceiling fan. Swaminathan sat next to VK, and his eyes were fixed on Pasha. Pasha found the room hot and suffocating, sweat trickling down his back under his shirt. He had been released from the jail sometime back, after serving time on dowry harassment charges, and being summoned for interrogation in the Jaishankar case did not make him particularly happy.

"He did," Pasha said, drinking from the glass of water which VK had pushed towards him.

VK asked, "Why did he call you, of all persons? We have checked and he hardly ever called even his own family!"

Pasha squirmed in his seat and said, "We got along well while we were in the jail together. I was in the barrack next to his. He mostly kept to himself. His family had already shunned him. The other inmates barely spoke to him. Maybe it had to do with the monstrosity of the crimes he had committed. I do not know if they feared him, or if they hated him. But Shankar and I got talking and had been in touch till the time he escaped from the jail."

"You did not hate him for his crimes, I assume?" asked VK.

Pasha took his time to answer. He was not sure where the Inspector was going with that question, and how his answer would be interpreted. He finally spoke. "You may find it strange, but speaking to Shankar never gave me the impression that he was this ruthless serial killer, who had raped and murdered more than two dozen women. He was like any of us. Like us, he wanted to be free. He had lived a trucker's life all along, moving across cities on open roads, and he felt claustrophobic, being holed up in his high security cell. Like us, he appeared weak and vulnerable. Sad, even, because everyone in the jail stayed away from him."

"What did you make of that?" Swaminathan bent forward and asked.

Pasha replied, "I *was* aware of the gruesome crimes he had committed, although I never brought up those incidents or fished for more information when I talked to him. Left to myself, I thought that there could be only two explanations for Shankar's behaviour. Either he was a very good actor, who was trying to win everyone's heart, or, there was indeed a dual personality at play. Maybe the Shankar I met and became friends with was really different from the sex-maniac that lay dormant while he was here. I would like to believe in the truth of the second theory. The Shankar I met was kind and friendly. I don't think that was an act he was putting on."

"You were released from the prison before his escape, weren't you?" asked VK.

"Yes, I was," replied Pasha.

"And Shankar stayed in touch," VK asked for conformation.

"Yes, he did. In fact, he had told me on the day I was released that he *would* stay in touch with me. He called me a few times from the jail after I had been released. I hope there was nothing wrong in talking to a friend," Pasha looked questioningly at the two policemen.

"Nothing wrong about that" VK nodded and asked. "Did he tell you anything about his plan of escaping from the jail? I can see from his call records that he called you three days before his escape."

"He never mentioned any such plan," Pasha replied confidently. "He did talk about getting in touch with me after he was *released*. I knew that he had already been convicted to ten years in prison in some of the cases in Karnataka, and he was being tried for more cases in the state, and then there were many more cases in the courts in Tamil Nadu. So, I was not sure about when he would actually be released from jail. In fact, I was not sure if he would ever be free! But I never told him that and humoured him when he talked about getting in touch with me after his release."

VK nodded and asked, "Did you meet him in the prison after your release?"

"Three times, to be exact," Pasha replied.

"Did you bring him presents?" asked Swaminathan.

"On a couple of occasions, I did," Pasha said. "Food, clean undergarments."

"Did you bring him a police uniform, or clothes that looked like one?"

Pasha wiped the sweat on his forehead and said, "No!"

"Did Shankar get in touch with you after his escape, asking for help?" asked VK. His eyes bored into the man sitting in front of him. Pasha felt vulnerable, stripped before the prying eyes of the hawk in front of him, its shadow now looming large over him.

He ran his tongue over his parched lips and said, "No, I have not heard from him after his escape from the prison. I read about the escape in the newspapers and heard the news bulletins on television. I have also seen the pamphlets at bus stops and grocery stores. But, trust me, I have no idea where Shankar is right now. He seems to have just vanished from the face of the earth."

The sky outside the only window in the room had turned dark. The trees tossed their heads in the breeze. The traffic could be heard on the busy road below.

VK bent over the table and brought his face close to Pasha's.

"Look here, Pasha! Don't try to act smart and be the benevolent friend to the most wanted criminal of the state. My order is simple. If you hear from Shankar, you must inform me. Let me warn you that if you choose to act otherwise, I will drag you back to jail on charges of helping a fugitive, and will make sure that you would be gone for long. Am I clearly understood?"

Pasha emptied the glass in front of him and nodded. His shirt now clung to his skin, drenched in sweat.

Chapter 39

6th September 2013

Vijay Kumar sat down by the lake. The water tanker he drove had been filled, and he could afford a couple of hours of rest before he hit the road again. The breeze made ripples on the surface of the lake and when it reached the shore, it felt cool and refreshing. Vijay rested his back against the trunk of a tree and stretched his legs. He brought his mobile phone out of his pocket. This might be a good time to call home, before he started on his journey. There were pockets in the highway where the connectivity was either weak or gone completely. He was about to light a cigarette and then make the call, when he noticed the man.

He had come out of the shack by the water. Vijay had earlier seen fishermen from the village resting inside that shack, but he did not recall having seen that man before. He was shabbily dressed, had close-cropped hair, and an emaciated appearance. It did not look like the man had had enough food or rest for several days. When the man began to walk in his direction, Vijay noticed that the man had bandages on his feet and limped. The man stooped as he walked, and he seemed to be in pain.

Vijay sat up straight. That man could be a junkie. He was definitely going to ask for money. One could not predict what the man would do if the money was denied. Vijay had heard stories of robberies and even murders being committed by addicts in these desolate areas.

"I am sorry to bother you," the man spoke in an unsure manner, "but can you please help me?"

The man was now standing at an arm's length from Vijay. Vijay noticed that the man had bruises all over, and there were blood stains on the bandages on his feet. The bugger must have been beaten up. Or, he might have had an accident.

The man seemed to have read his mind.

He smiled with some difficulty, revealing yellow-brown teeth, and said, "I am not sure who you think I am, but let me assure you that I mean no harm. I am a bus driver. I was driving from Tamil Nadu along the state highway a few days back. The bus met with an accident. Trust me, it was not my fault. A car had come from the wrong direction at a hundred-plus. My bus rammed into it, even before I could apply the brakes." The man paused and took a deep breath. It seemed to Vijay that the man had not recovered from the shock of the accident.

"Did anyone die?" Vijay asked the man.

The man bowed his head and nodded. "The man who was driving the car did not make it. There was another man inside the bus, sitting next to my seat, who died as well." The man looked at Vijay and smiled wryly. "I was injured, but managed to escape. I have been hiding since then in this shack by the lake. I am afraid that the police will not let me go if they get their hands on me." Vijay nodded his head. He knew what the man meant. The man went on, "I did not have a lot of money on myself. Whatever little I had, I have already spent on treatment and food."

Vijay could imagine what was coming next. However, the man surprised him. He did not ask for money. Instead, the man said, "Can I use your mobile phone for calling a friend? I need food, some money and a motorbike to leave this place. I am sure he will bail me out."

Just one phone call. That was all that the man was asking for. And it surely was not too much. Vijay handed the phone over to him. The man took the phone from Vijay with a look of heartfelt gratitude on his face. For the first time, Vijay felt sorry for him.

The man dialled a number from memory and pressed the phone to his ear. He listened to the phone ringing on the other end of the line so intently that it seemed as if his life depended on that one call. Well, it actually did.

When his friend took the call, the man's tired face lit up in an instant. He smiled from ear to ear and said, "Pasha? This is Shankar!"

"Shankar, how are you? Where have you been all these days? You are all over the news, my friend! And whose number is this? Where are you calling from?" Shankar was bombarded with questions.

"Pasha, I have been hiding from the police here in a village in Kudlu Gate. I was badly injured and could not go far. But I have run out of money, and I need to get out of this place. Can you help me?" the man begged. Vijay kept listening to the conversation. He was now curious and was hoping that the poor fellow did manage to escape.

"Of course I will help you, Shankar. What are friends for?" said Pasha, "Tell me where exactly I should meet you with the bike and the money."

Shankar blurted off details of his location.

"I will call you back at this number in the next thirty minutes and confirm," said Pasha before ending the call.

Shankar returned the phone to Vijay and said, "Thank you so much, brother. My friend will call back at this number in the next half-an-hour. Will you be kind enough to wait here till then?" There were tears in the man's eyes as he spoke.

"I will wait," Vijay put a hand on the man's shoulder and smiled. He could surely wait for the next thirty minutes.

"I cannot thank you enough!" said the man.

***

As soon as he had finished the conversation with Shankar, Pasha dialled the number of Inspector V.K. Singh.

The bounty of five lakhs was now just waiting to be grabbed!

Chapter 40

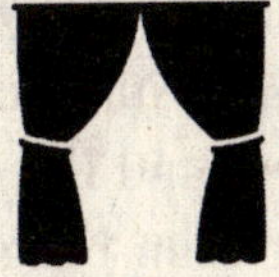

"Shankar is hiding in a fisherman's hut by the Nagendra Reddy Lake in Kudlu Gate. It's only about six kilometres from the Central Prison," VK looked around the room as he put the receiver down. He paced up and down the room and continued, "Shankar called Pasha for help a while back using someone else's mobile phone. He asked for a motorbike, money and food. Pasha passed on the number to me, and I called the man whose phone Shankar had used. He drives a water tanker and he met Shankar near the lake. His name is Vijay Kumar. I pretended to be Pasha's loyal friend, and told Vijay that we would be there soon with everything that Shankar had asked for. Shankar must stay put right there."

VK turned to Inspector Ashok, who was the City Crime Branch chief, and said, "Get your boys ready. We must send a team to the spot right now! I want you to lead the mission."

***

The man did not budge an inch even for a second and kept sitting next to Vijay for the next twenty-five minutes till the phone rang. The number was different from the one which the man had dialled. The voice on the other side delivered a message that was short – "Inform your friend that we are on our way to Kudlu Gate with a motorbike that Pasha has arranged for him. We are also bringing along some food and cash, as your friend requested. He must not go anywhere." Vijay conveyed the message to the man, looking at him with surprise and admiration. The wretched bugger had contacts in all the right places! How else could one get money and a motorbike arranged in minutes? The man, on the other hand, seemed to finally breathe, on hearing the news. He dragged himself along the grass and rested his back against the trunk of the tree. Despite his apparent physical pain, he looked relaxed.

"Where are you planning to go? It does not look like you would be able to ride on a bike too far from here," said Vijay as he took a puff of the beedi. He offered one to the man, who readily grabbed the stick and took a long drag with his eyes closed, as if he had been craving for that one drag all his life.

"You are right. My back is in bad shape. I am not sure how far I would be able to go. Also, I cannot risk travelling during the day. I have to wait for it to be dark," said the man absent-mindedly. He turned towards Vijay and said, "I will always be grateful to you, my friend."

Vijay smiled. He wondered if he had done the right thing by helping the man to escape. Well, if the man was to be believed, the accident had not been his fault. The car had been charging down the highway in the wrong direction! The man could not be held responsible for the loss of two lives. Vijay assured himself that he had not broken the law by helping the man. He had to leave soon. He decided to hang around till the man he had spoken to on the phone reached the spot and handed the bike over to the poor fellow, and then he would leave. It had been an unusual experience so far. He wanted to see how the story ended.

Before long, they could hear voices at a distance. "I think they are here," the man grinned, and tried to get up.

***

Inspector Ashok moved ahead, followed by his force. There was not much of cover, but the police tried to be as discrete as possible, hiding behind the trunks of tall trees and thick bushes. The only sound was that of heavy boots trudging on the grass and dry leaves. The relentless croaking of frogs by the lake seemed to underline the silence of the dusk. Dark clouds drifted across the sky.

Inspector Ashok could see the hut at a distance through the thick foliage. The pathway that led to the hut was overgrown with weeds. One of the officers whispered in his ears, "That must be the place, sir. It was built as a resting place by the lake for fishermen. Shankar could not have found a better place to hide in this village. There is no other house in its vicinity."

As Inspector Ashok looked closely, he could see two men sitting under a tree by the hut.

Shankar's attire and appearance gave him away immediately. It was not difficult to figure out that the other man was the driver of the water tanker. Shankar must have called Pasha using that man's phone. The water tanker itself could be seen at a short distance from the lake.

Inspector Ashok gestured at four of his officers to surround the hut at the back and on two sides in case Shankar decided to make a run for it. He himself walked in brisk steps towards the two men, a hand firmly placed on the butt of the gun in his holster.

Vijay jumped up when he saw Inspector Ashok. Shankar tried to stand, but his legs gave away. He then tried to crawl towards the hut, but Ashok already had his gun trained on the fugitive.

"Your game is up, Shankar!" roared Ashok. "Do not even think about escaping. You are surrounded by the police on all sides."

Shankar froze, as the pain in his back sent shockwaves throughout his body. "Pasha, motherfucker, you gave me up to the police!" Shankar muttered under his breath.

Ashok smiled and said, "This is precisely why we must choose our friends wisely!" as he handcuffed Shankar.

***

In no time, the village was abuzz with the news of the arrest of the dreaded 'psycho killer'. The villagers were shocked when the news spread like wildfire. The stranger who had been living in the area for the past five days was none other than Jaishankar!

"We used to see him moving around here and there, but we never imagined that he was the dreaded criminal the police were looking for all over the state. Thank god, he was injured, and the police managed to catch him soon. Otherwise, going by his track record, anything could have happened to our daughters," said an old man from the village to a reporter.

"I had no idea that I had lent my phone to a fugitive, and that too, none other than Psycho Shankar!" said Vijay Kumar to the reporters. "I get goosebumps when I think of the time I spent with him, sitting under that tree, smoking beedis and waiting for someone to turn up with a motorbike on which he would escape!"

***

When Chief Minister Siddaramaiah was informed that Bangalore police had nabbed the convicted serial rapist and killer Jaishankar, he did not believe it initially. He asked the person who broke the news to him if the arrest had really been made. *"Nijavagiyu arrest madidara?"*

When the caller confirmed, the incredulous chief minister repeated, *"Nijvagiyu avananna hididhidara?"* (Has *he* really been arrested?)

It was only after city Police Commissioner Manavendra Agarkar called him and assured him that Shankar was in police custody did the chief minister believe that the fugitive was indeed behind bars. The chief minister finally breathed a sigh of relief.

***

"Shankar wanted a motorbike to escape to Tamil Nadu. It would have been very difficult to catch him, had he reached the highways. We are proud of the team led by Inspector V.K. Singh, ADGP K.V. Amandeep and Inspector Ashok from the City Crime Branch, that caught him while he was still in hiding six kilometres from the jail from which he had escaped. He sustained injuries in his legs and arms while escaping from the prison. He is also complaining of back pain. The specialist doctors in the police will look into those injuries," said Commissioner Agarkar in the press meet. He turned towards Inspector Swaminathan and said, "I would like to especially thank Inspector Swaminathan for helping us understand the psychology of the killer and predicting his actions, thanks to his long involvement in the cases against M. Jaishankar. He is the one who suggested that we should intensify our search in the areas in the vicinity of the Central Jail, and instead of focusing on his family and friends, keep an eye on those with whom he had been in touch from the prison of late and was likely to reach out for help after his escape."

Swaminathan smiled and lowered his head in acknowledgement. For the last five years, his life had mostly been about getting Shankar behind bars and keeping him there. He wondered for how many more years Shankar would keep him on his toes!

***

After being remanded to judicial custody, Shankar was admitted to Victoria Hospital for medical treatment. Additional Commissioner of Police (Law and Order) Amal Pant was not happy. "We will protest this decision and take legal course to obtain his custody. We are yet to conduct a detailed interrogation and are expecting some answers on how he managed to escape from Central Prison," he said.

It was decided that ADGP Amandeep and Inspector V.K. Singh would continue the investigation into the circumstances in which Shankar managed to escape from the Central Prison. They would be interrogating the eleven officials who had earlier been suspended pending inquiry. Whether Shankar received help in escaping from the prison and whether there was any insider involvement were the questions uppermost in the minds of the investigators. It was still to be ascertained how Shankar had got hold of the crude key which he had used to open the lock of his cell in the hospital block. Also, the fact that the supply of electricity to the barbwire on the perimeter walls had been cut off was also quite mysterious.

***

On 13th March 2014, Chief Secretary Kaushik Mukherjee and Director-General and Inspector General of Police, Lalrokhuma Pachau presented a cheque worth five lakhs to Pasha at a function organised at Malleswaram grounds in Bangalore.

The police did not entertain the claim of Vijay Kumar that he had also helped them nab Shankar. "Vijay was not helpful for us in finding Jaishankar, or in any other form during the investigation, as he was not even aware that he had met Jaishankar on Friday, when we actually arrested him," a senior officer who was a part of the investigating team said.

Needless to say, Vijay Kumar was not satisfied with that answer.

Chapter 41

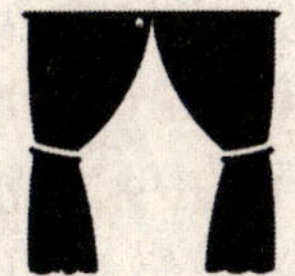

"Come back, girls!" Shankar gasped, "I cannot run anymore!"

He stood in the middle of the pathway that cut through the forest on both sides, trying to catch his breath, his head lowered, his hands on his aching knees. His daughters had outrun him as usual and were nowhere to be seen. They were growing up fast, and their appa was not getting any younger. His bones were aching, and his joints creaking. Shankar realised right at that moment that he was too old for those frivolous games with his daughters.

Daylight was slowly ebbing and the forest was getting cold. Shankar knew that it was going to be a long walk back home. Rajeshwari must be worried, and he surely was in for an earful for being an irresponsible father. "Come back, girls!" Shankar called them wearily one more time. Then, he started trudging along the dusty road to find his daughters, his eyes hovering on the thick bushes that lined the road. They must be hiding behind one of those!

He stopped when he noticed some movement behind a bush to his right. That part of the forest was dark and damp.

The sun had set, and cacophonous flocks of birds made strange patterns in the sky as they flew homewards. Shankar made his way through the tall grass and reached behind the thick bush. What he saw with his unbelieving eyes made him freeze. His mouth opened, but the scream was buried in his throat. He saw his three daughters lying dead on the ground, their clothes drenched in blood, their faces disfigured. Standing near them was a man, looking formidable in his long moustache and flowing hair, his devilish laughter echoing in the forest. He was carrying a machete, its blade stained with the blood of his three daughters. The black bag near the man's feet looked familiar. The machete looked familiar. So did the man.

That man was Shankar himself!

Shankar cried out and woke up from his dream, the dream that kept coming back to haunt him every time he closed his eyes. He was drenched in sweat and his throat felt dry.

He tried to remember when he had seen his daughters for the last time.

***

Shankar was sent back to the Parappana Agrahara prison (Bangalore Central Jail) after the successful operation on his fractured leg at the Victoria Hospital on 23rd September 2013, the procedure costing the government seventy-five thousand rupees. The amount, added to the bounty of five lakhs which the state paid to Pasha, made Shankar's escape from the Central Prison a costly affair indeed!

He was put up in a high-security cell. There was a CCTV monitoring him, and a guard kept an eye on him round the clock. The injuries he had sustained while escaping from the Central Prison had made it difficult for Shankar to move around without a wheelchair and his treatment at the Victoria and Bowring hospitals continued for more than a month. Because of his immobility, another inmate was permitted to assist him.

The police had learnt costly lessons from his earlier escapades. They made sure that the lock in his prison cell was well out of his reach, so that he could not open the lock and sneak out of his cell, like he had done the last time he was in the Central Prison. If he complained of illness, a doctor would attend to him inside the cell, and he would not be shifted to a hospital. Also, whenever he was taken to a court for a hearing, extra security was deployed to make sure that there was no repetition of the incident at the Salem bus depot in 2011.

As the police continued the probe into the circumstances that led to Shankar's escape from the prison, they had to carry him to several places. Among the people whom Shankar used to call from the jail, the police had identified a truck driver, who was Shankar's elder brother. "I lost all hopes of coming out of jail and made up my mind that I had to escape. I spoke to my elder brother. He promised that he would help me go to Haryana. I planned to take my family along, and find a job there," Shankar said, when the police asked him why he had escaped from the prison.

Shankar did not have visitors in jail. His family had abandoned him several years back. He had no friends. He was also paranoid that his fellow inmates might attack him, as he had been a serial rapist. He was aware that rapists were not treated kindly by prisoners in a jail, and they were vulnerable to attacks. He, therefore, barely moved out of his cell. On rare occasions, he moved around the jail premises on his wheelchair, assuring himself that the 'righteous' prisoners who regularly beat up rapists might spare a physically handicapped convict.

Shankar did not speak to anyone. In his mind, he had figured out that everyone was out to get him – the police, the politicians, his family, his so-called friends. Therefore, he had no reason to be friendly with them. He had taken Pasha's betrayal to heart.

On the earlier occasions when Shankar had been in prison, while the effects of imprisonment had definitely taken their toll on his body and mind, his spirit had not been crushed and he had not felt empty and defeated. Shankar remembered that the first time he had been thrown behind bars, he had been scared. He had even considered killing himself before he was sent to jail. He had been scared that he would be beaten up by other convicts, maybe even sodomised. In the early days in jail, he had gone through hell. He had cried through the nights. He had been a wreck. But he had got over that phase. He had learnt to cope with the system, and then to fight against it, as he had resolved that he would not tear himself apart. After a short while, he had not let his fears and his vulnerabilities control him or destroy him. He had managed to survive, and to escape on both occasions.

This time, however, Shankar felt that he was sinking deeper and deeper, into a never-ending chasm of hopelessness. He was fast losing his mind. He was also heart-broken due to the fact that the courts were convicting him in most of the cases, barring a few like the case in Namakkal in Tamil Nadu, where Shankar had been tried for 'allegedly' dismembering and hacking to death with a sickle a fifty-year-old woman after she had been raped and robbed in September 2009, and he had been acquitted five years later as the police had failed to produce adequate evidence, thanks to a botched-up investigation.

No amount of treatment for depression, meditation and yoga exercises were going to help. Shankar stood like a bystander watching the days melt into weeks and the weeks into months, even as he kept battling the demons inside him – roguish, invincible – that made deafening noises inside his head all through his waking hours, and then tormented him in his dreams when he slept. Shankar knew that he had fathered those demons himself, and now he had to carry them around inside him all his life.

The only conversations he had were with his doctor who was treating him for his depression, Dr S.R. Prasanna.

The doctor was surprised how the man had an answer ready for every question he was asked during his therapy sessions.

***

"Do you ever feel any remorse for the fact that while those women you killed were strangers for you, they had families and loved ones who had the right to know where you had disposed off their bodies?" asked the doctor.

"Once I killed a woman, there was nothing that I could do to bring her back. There was nothing I could do to reduce the pain of her loved ones. Would it be better for her loved ones to know that she had been reduced to a pile of bones lying somewhere? Or, even worse? Would it not be easier for them to live with the hope that she would be back someday?" replied Shankar.

"Did you ever make an honest attempt to mend your ways?"

"I have always felt like there is a darker side to me, which overshadows my normal life. I have always been aware of the possible consequences of what I have been doing. Those senseless, inhuman, cruel acts are illegal. People lose their freedom when they are arrested for such crimes. Like I now have. I would really like to understand the motives behind my behaviour and eliminate them completely. But you know what? I never got to understand those motives in the first place. So, it does not matter if I want to change or not. I do not know if I can at all make a choice about who I want to be," Shankar almost sounded regretful. "I would love to recognise what caused me to act the way I did and how to deal with those urges. I would love to go to a place that did not exert upon me the stress or the pressure that aroused those feelings of anger, hostility, insecurity, low self-esteem, and lust. But I do not know if such a place even exists."

"How did you really feel when you committed those crimes?"

"I committed a lot of those crimes in a state of intoxication, so I do not remember minute details. For the rest, I can recollect exactly how I felt. At each stage of the act, my feelings were different. Compare this with a hunting expedition. The feeling of sighting an animal for the first time would be different from actually shooting it or carrying the dead animal home with you or butchering and cleaning it up or having it for dinner. At every stage, the emotions are different. So, it is very difficult to put my finger on exactly one emotion that I went through during each of those incidents."

"How does it feel to be branded a monster?"

"You see, I am really not concerned about my image anymore. It is terrible, anyway. I know who I am, where I came from, how I grew up. I know that I had an identity different from the monster that I have become. But none of that matters now. And I feel no need to relate to people or impress them. I do not care about my reputation. Given a choice, I would love to be the most obscure person in the world right now, hiding somewhere."

"Do you realise that you may be sentenced to death?"

"Yes, and I am surprised. The death penalty is nothing but the need of the state and the victims' families to take revenge on me. An eye for an eye. You see, the society condones a lot of killing, often on a massive scale. In a war. By the way of abortion. Even the slaughter of animals for food. But, if the society has the love and respect for life, it cannot be selective about how it honours that love and respect. You cannot have love for a two-year-old, but be okay with killing a foetus! You cannot have love for a puppy but be okay with feasting on a lamb! Likewise, you cannot have respect for the victim's life, and kill the murderer! If the life of the victim was sacred, so is the life of the killer. This inconsistency puzzles me. It is because of this inconsistency that in a way, the society and the law are self-generating violence. In a never-ending loop."

The doctor was left speechless.

***

On the morning of Sunday, 25th February 2018, the nation woke up to the shocking news of the death of its heartthrob, the legendary actress, Sridevi in Dubai. On the same day, Shankar – now sentenced in three cases in Tamil Nadu and under trial for twelve more cases, nine in Tamil Nadu and three in Karnataka, and already serving a jail term of around thirty-two years – made a half-hearted attempt to escape from the Bangalore Central Prison once again, his handicap notwithstanding. However, luck did not favour him on that occasion.

Instead, he was thrown into solitary confinement, and the security measures were beefed up.

No one knew that Shankar was planning for another escape. A fool proof one.

Chapter 42

27th February 2018

Vetrivel had been upset since he had heard the news of Sridevi's passing away. He was a die-hard fan. As he sat outside the high-security cell of the serial killer looking at the wallpaper of his mobile phone from where Sri smiled back at him, he remembered the one time he had seen the diva at an arm's length when she had come for the premier of one of her movies in Bangalore. He remembered how he had bunked classes in college to watch her movies. He took his girlfriend along to watch *Himmatwala* on their first date. Sri had been an integral part of all his precious memories like millions of Indians, and now he found it hard to believe that she was no more! It seemed to Vetrivel that the world would not be the same without Sri and her movies. The daughter, of course, showed promise. But would she be able to fill her mother's shoes? Only time would tell.

He was pulled out of his reverie by muffled cries inside the cell.

He stood up in a flash. It was past two in the night, and the man should ideally be asleep. Where were those sounds coming from? You could never predict what the devil was up to! Only a couple of days back, he had tried to escape from the Central Prison for the second time, with that broken spine and fractured leg.

Vetrivel opened the door of the cell, and his jaw dropped!

Shankar was lying in a pool of blood and convulsing, the deep gash in his neck spewing blood incessantly.

Vetrivel immediately ran off to get help.

Even as he writhed in pain and could feel life slowly ebbing away, Shankar silently thanked the barber who had given him the shaving blade the day before. This worthless life was not worth living anymore! This was going to be his grand escape. This time, for good.

For a fleeting second, he remembered the face of the Inspector from Tirupur, Swaminathan, always ready to rush to any corner of the world to bring him back to jail. He wondered how the Inspector would feel, now that he had had the last laugh.

***

Shankar was first taken to the jail hospital where he was administered first aid, but within the next hour, his condition worsened. He had lost a lot of blood and his vitals were steadily deteriorating. He was immediately rushed to the Victoria Hospital.

Psycho Shankar, terror of the highways, prisoner number 5483, passed away at ten minutes past five in the morning at the Victoria Hospital, leaving behind the serpentine roads he had once ruled, the farms still stained by the blood of his innocent victims, the air thick with the stink of rotting flesh, the warm winds carrying across arid fields by the roads the helpless wails of the women he had mercilessly violated and butchered.

Chapter 43

The police had no idea how Shankar had managed to get hold of a blade, unnoticed, within the high-security cell under CCTV surveillance. And then, how could he use that blade to commit suicide inside the heavily guarded cell? As if the lapses from the last time Shankar had escaped from the Central Prison had not been enough to strike a telling blow on the credibility and sincerity of the police, there was now his suicide to rub salt to the wound.

The Parappana Agrahara police filed a case for investigation. A special team was constituted to look into the matter.

***

In the next two days, no one from Shankar's family turned up to receive his body. Shankar's body was kept in the mortuary of Victoria Hospital, awaiting post-mortem and cremation. The Bangalore Central Prison police, while taking up a case of unnatural death, was kept waiting for his immediate family, relatives or friends to come forward and complete the necessary formalities, but no one, it seemed, was interested in the deceased man's last rites.

The police got in touch with their counterparts in Tamil Nadu to approach the family, considering his wife, three daughters, elder brother and elder sister were from that state. When the local police contacted Shankar's family, they initially declined to receive his body. The local police checked again at the insistence of Bangalore police. It was also suggested that if the family was not willing to receive the body, then they should issue a written statement to that effect. Once the police in Bangalore received that letter from the family, they would continue with the formalities. They were willing to wait for a day or two more, in case the family had a change of mind. If the family did not change its mind, then the Bangalore police would go ahead with the autopsy, which had to be conducted in the presence of a magistrate since Shankar had been a convict. The police would then also perform the last rites.

Finally, on Friday night, more than three days after Shankar's death, his wife Rajeshwari arrived in Bangalore along with her father.

***

Rajeshwari, who now worked as a daily wager in Tamil Nadu, was shocked when she received the news of Shankar's death. The first reaction of the family was to distance itself from the dead convict. Also, as word got around, the villagers assembled at her door. They would not allow the family to bring Shankar's mortal remains to the village. He was the devil reincarnated. They would never allow the soil of the village to be sullied by a man who had, throughout his life, raped and killed innumerable women.

Finally, Palaniswamy, Rajeshwari's father intervened. "At least have mercy on his daughters! They want to see their father one last time," he said. His pleas finally made the family and the villagers relent.

When the old man and his daughter reached Bangalore, the autopsy on Shankar's body was completed at Victoria Hospital, and the body was ready to be handed over to the family.

When Rajeshwari saw the man lying dead before her, she felt numb. For the first few minutes, she felt nothing at all. Then, she felt angry and wanted to scream her lungs out at that man. Finally, sadness crept up from somewhere deep inside her heart and made its way to her eyes, squeezing through the rage and the hatred, as she remembered the virile young man of twenty-three, whom she had married many springs back with her eyes filled with dreams that would eventually turn out to be just that – dreams.

***

When Inspector Swaminathan heard the news of Shankar's suicide, he was in his office. He kept staring at the phone in disbelief, long after he had put the receiver down. For the last ten years, his life had only been about getting into the twisted mind of that man, hunting him down every time he managed to evade the long arm of the law, battling it out in the courts, and holding on to his faith in the judicial system.

He celebrated every time that man was convicted. He sank into despair every time that man was acquitted in a trial.

And now, that man was gone forever, escaping the gallows.

Swaminathan felt that destiny had provided the monster with a short cut on his way out of a life of ignominy, humiliation and misery in prison. That was anything but fair. That was not fair to the dozens of women who had been devoured on the roads and left to rot far away from their homes. That was not fair to their families and loved ones for whom the last and the lasting memories of their daughters, sisters, wives and lovers were the leftovers of flesh and bones ravaged by animals, birds, insects and the weather. They would never have the closure they so badly needed. Over the last decade, Swaminathan had devoted himself to that sole purpose in life – to bring these families closure and justice.

And now, that purpose was gone. He felt empty inside.

His eyes welled up, and his fingers curled into a fist. He kept banging his desk in the empty room as daylight faded outside the window.

References

1. "M. Jaishankar" - Wikipedia (https://en.wikipedia.org/wiki/M._Jaishankar)
2. "Psycho Shankar - How the serial rapist and killer was nabbed" - India News (https://www.indiatoday.in/india/south/story/psycho-shankar-how-serial-rapist-killer-was-nabbed-210165-2013-09-06)
3. "Serial rape convict 'Psycho Jaishankar' slits own throat, kills self in Bengaluru Central Prison" - The New Indian Express (https://www.newindianexpress.com/cities/bengaluru/2018/feb/27/serial-rape-convict-psycho-jaishankar-slits-own-throat-kills-self-in-bengaluru-central-prison-1779622.html)
4. "Serial rapist Jaishankar found dead in jail cell at Bengaluru Central Prison" - The Hindu (https://www.thehindu.com/news/national/karnataka/serial-rapist-jaishankar-found-dead-in-jail-cell-at-bengaluru-central-prison/article22870911.ece)
5. "Criminal rapes, kills 6 women after escape from Salem" - Chennai News, Times of India (https://timesofindia.indiatimes.com/city/chennai/Criminal-rapes-kills-6-women-after-escape-from-Salem/articleshow/8103461.cms)
6. "Bed-ridden and 'lonely' rapist Psycho Shankar slits his throat" (https://bangaloremirror.indiatimes.com/bangalore/crime/bed-ridden-and-lonely-rapist-psycho-shankar-slits-his-throat/articleshow/63100037.cms)
7. "M Shankar alias Jaishankar has no control over criminal instinct" - Bengaluru News, Times of India (https://timesofindia.indiatimes.com/city/bengaluru/M-Shankar-alias-Jaishankar-has-no-control-over-criminal-instinct/articleshow/22217646.cms)

8. "Namakkal Court Acquits Jaishankar in Murder Case" – The New Indian Express (https://www.newindianexpress.com/states/karnataka/2014/feb/01/Namakkal-Court-Acquits-Jaishankar-in-Murder-Case-570922.html)
9. "Serial rapist-killer Jaishankar planned escape over two months" – Bengaluru News, Times of India (https://timesofindia.indiatimes.com/city/bengaluru/Serial-rapist-killer-Jaishankar-planned-escape-over-two-months/articleshow/22382895.cms)
10. "A life in crime: Rapist-killer who terrorised women on highways" – India News, The Indian Express (https://indianexpress.com/article/india/a-life-in-crime-rapist-killer-who-terrorised-women-on-highways-m-jaishankar-5083411/)
11. "M. Jaishankar: The Terror of Psycho Shankar that Traumatized Civilians" – Forensic Yard (https://forensicyard.com/the-terror-of-psycho-jaishankar/)
12. "Who was Psycho Shankar? Know about serial killer, rapist M Jaishankar dead in Bengaluru prison" – The Financial Express (https://www.financialexpress.com/india-news/who-was-psycho-shankar-know-about-serial-killer-rapist-m-jaishankar-dead-in-bengaluru-prison/1083263/)
13. "Real Ratsasan: The Story of Psycho Shankar" – Ulagam (https://astroulagam.com.my/lifestyle/real-ratsasan-story-psycho-shankar-82968)
14. "Woman constable's body found near Tirupur" – The New Indian Express (https://www.newindianexpress.com/states/tamil-nadu/2009/sep/19/woman-constables-body-found-near-tirupur-87592.html)
15. "Stalin guard found murdered" (https://bangaloremirror.indiatimes.com/news/india/stalin-guard-found-murdered/articleshow/22042425.cms)

16. "Dangerous and free: 'Serial killer rapist' has police on edge" – Deccan Herald (https://www.deccanherald.com/amp/content/354748/dangerous-free-serial-killer-rapist.html)
17. "How Bangalore police caught psycho Shankar" (https://www.news18.com/news/india/shankar-637143.html)
18. "Constable rape and murder case mba advt P.Chandrasekaran 482 direction petition" – sekarreporter.com 9445430817 (https://wwwsekarreporter.wordpress.com/2018/02/07/constable-rape-and-murder-case-mba-advt-p-chandrasekaran-482-direction-petition/)
19. "Constable kills himself after accused in custody escapes" – Coimbatore News, Times of India (https://timesofindia.indiatimes.com/city/coimbatore/constable-kills-himself-after-accused-in-custody-escapes/articleshow/7745799.cms)
20. "Accused escapes, constable shoots self" – The Hindu (https://www.thehindu.com/news/national/tamil-nadu/Accused-escapes-constable-shoots-self/article14953751.ece)
21. "Undertrial escape: Armed reserve constable commits suicide" – The Hindu (https://www.thehindu.com/news/cities/Coimbatore/Undertrial-escape-Armed-reserve-constable-commits-suicide/article14953640.ece)
22. "Jaishankar" – Murderpedia, the encyclopedia of murderers (https://murderpedia.org/male.J/j/jaishankar.htm)
23. "Convict jumps City central prison" – Deccan Herald (https://www.deccanherald.com/content/354740/convict-jumps-city-central-prison.html)
24. "Police launch manhunt for serial rapist" – India News, The Indian Express (https://indianexpress.com/article/india/india-others/police-launch-manhunt-for-serial-rapist/)
25. Abdul Nazer Mahdani – Wikipedia (https://en.wikipedia.org/wiki/Abdul_Nazer_Mahdani)

26. "Man who helped police nab Jaishankar rewarded" – The Hindu (https://www.thehindu.com/news/cities/bangalore//article60403062.ece)
27. "Fugitive Jaishankar caught a few km from central jail" – The Hindu (https://www.thehindu.com/news/cities/bangalore//article60428033.ece)
28. "Jaishankar remanded in police custody" – The Hindu (https://www.thehindu.com/news/cities/bangalore//article60427898.ece)
29. "Jaishankar remanded in police custody" – The Hindu (https://www.dailymail.co.uk/indiahome/indianews/article-2414340/Jaishankar-The-fugitive-caught-police-escaping-Bangalore-Central-Prison.html)
30. "Rs 5 lakh reward for man who helped police apprehend Jaishankar" – Deccan Herald (https://www.deccanherald.com/content/391889/rs-5-lakh-reward-man.html)
31. "Initially, CM didn't believe cops had caught Jaishankar" (https://bangaloremirror.indiatimes.com/bangalore/crime/serial-rapist-jaishankar/articleshow/22401187.cms)
32. "Jaishankar slipped out between hospital and cell" – Bengaluru News, Times of India (https://timesofindia.indiatimes.com/city/bengaluru/jaishankar-slipped-out-between-hospital-and-cell/articleshow/22352026.cms)
33. "Informant was key to fugitive's arrest" – The New Indian Express (https://www.newindianexpress.com/cities/bengaluru/2013/sep/07/Informant-was-key-to-fugitives-arrest-514236.html)
34. "Escaped rape convict still untraceable" – The New Indian Express (https://www.newindianexpress.com/cities/bengaluru/2013/sep/05/Escaped-rape-convict-still-untraceable-513660.html)

35. "False alarm keeps cops on their toes" – Indian Express (http://archive.indianexpress.com/news/false-alarm-keeps-cops-on-their-toes/1164363/)
36. "Residents shocked over Jaishankar's presence in Kudlu" – Kannadiga World (https://www.kannadigaworld.com/news/karnataka/35010.html)
37. Bangalore jail: An island of the unwanted – Deccan Herald (https://www.deccanherald.com/content/86904/bangalore-jail-island-unwanted.html)
38. "5 days on, runaway serial rapist still at large, jail staff under lens" (https://www.dailypioneer.com/2013/india/5-days-on-runaway-serial-rapist-still-at-large-jail-staff-under-lens.html)
39. "Rs 75k spent on serial rapist-killer's surgery" (https://bangaloremirror.indiatimes.com/bangalore/crime/rapist-killer-surgery-bangalore-news/articleshowprint/23114115.cms?prtpage=1)
40. "'Psycho' Shankar was immobile after Bengaluru's Parappana Agrahara jail break" – The New Indian Express (https://www.newindianexpress.com/cities/bengaluru/2018/feb/28/psycho-shankar-was-immobile-after-bengalurus-parappana-agrahara-jail-break-1779902.html)
41. "Kin not willing to collect 'Psycho' Shankar's body" – The New Indian Express (https://www.newindianexpress.com/states/karnataka/2018/mar/01/kin-not-willing-to-collect-psycho-shankars-body-1780405.html)